THE PILGRIM'S REGRESS

Davis

It's about the island? (heaven?)

By the same Author

MIRACLES

THE SCREWTAPE LETTERS

THE PROBLEM OF PAIN

TRANSPOSITION

BROADCAST TALKS

CHRISTIAN BEHAVIOUR

BEYOND PERSONALITY

THE GREAT DIVORCE

GEORGE MACDONALD—ANTHOLOGY

THE ABOLITION OF MAN

THE
PILGRIM'S REGRESS

An Allegorical Apology for Christianity
Reason and Romanticism

by

C. S. LEWIS

As cold waters to a thirsty soul,
so is good news from a far country.
—*Proverbs*

GEOFFREY BLES
52 DOUGHTY STREET, LONDON

First published in 1933
New and revised edition 1943
Seventh edition 1950

To
ARTHUR GREEVES

PRINTED IN GREAT BRITAIN BY ROBERT MACLEHOSE AND CO. LTD.
THE UNIVERSITY PRESS, GLASGOW

PREFACE TO THIRD EDITION

ON re-reading this book ten years after I wrote it, I find its chief faults to be those two which I myself least easily forgive in the books of other men: needless obscurity, and an uncharitable temper.

There were two causes, I now realise, for the obscurity. On the intellectual side my own progress had been from 'popular realism' to Philosophical Idealism; from Idealism to Pantheism; from Pantheism to Theism; and from Theism to Christianity. I still think this a very natural road, but I now know that it is a road very rarely trodden. In the early thirties I did not know this. If I had had any notion of my own isolation, I should either have kept silent about my journey or else endeavoured to describe it with more consideration for the reader's difficulties. As things were, I committed the same sort of blunder as one who should narrate his travels through the Gobi Desert on the assumption that this route was as familiar to the British public as the line from Euston to Crewe. And this original blunder was soon aggravated by a profound change in the philosophical thought of our age. Idealism itself went out of fashion. The dynasty of Green, Bradley, and Bosanquet fell, and the world inhabited by philosophical students of my own generation became as alien to our successors as if not years but centuries had intervened.

The second cause of obscurity was the (unintentionally) 'private' meaning I then gave to the word 'Romanticism'. I would not now use this word to describe the experience which is central in this book. I would not, indeed, use it to describe anything, for I now believe it to be a word of such varying senses that it has become useless and should be banished from our vocabulary. Even if we exclude the vulgar sense in which a 'romance' means simply 'a love affair' (Peer and Film Star Romance) I think we can distinguish at least seven kinds of things which are called 'romantic'.

1. Stories about dangerous adventure—particularly, dangerous adventure in the past or in remote places—are 'romantic'. In this sense Dumas is a typically 'romantic' author, and stories about sailing

5

14335

ships, the Foreign Legion, and the rebellion of 1745, are usually 'romantic'.

2. The marvellous is 'romantic', provided it does not make part of the believed religion. Thus magicians, ghosts, fairies, witches, dragons, nymphs, and dwarfs are 'romantic'; angels, less so. Greek gods are 'romantic' in Mr. James Stephens or Mr. Maurice Hewlett; not so in Homer and Sophocles. In this sense Malory, Boiardo, Ariosto, Spenser, Tasso, Mrs. Radcliffe, Shelley, Coleridge, William Morris, and Mr. E. R. Eddison are 'romantic' authors.

3. The art dealing with 'Titanic' characters, emotions strained beyond the common pitch, and high-flown sentiments or codes of honour is 'romantic'. (I welcome the growing use of the word 'Romanesque' to describe this type.) In this sense Rostand and Sidney are 'romantic', and so (though unsuccessfully) are Dryden's Heroic Dramas, and there is a good deal of 'romanticism' in Corneille. I take it that Michelangelo is, in this sense, a 'romantic' artist.

4. 'Romanticism' can also mean the indulgence in abnormal, and finally in anti-natural, moods. The *macabre* is 'romantic', and so is an interest in torture, and a love of death. This, if I understand them, is what M. Mario Praz and M. D. de Rougemont would mean by the word. In this sense *Tristan* is Wagner's most 'romantic' opera; Poe, Baudelaire, and Flaubert, are 'romantic' authors; Surrealism is 'romantic'.

5. Egoism and Subjectivism are 'romantic'. In this sense the typically 'romantic' books are *Werther* and Rousseau's *Confessions*, and the works of Byron and Proust.

6. Every revolt against existing civilisation and conventions whether it look forward to revolution, or backward to the 'primitive' is called 'romantic' by some people. Thus pseudo-Ossian, Epstein, D. H. Lawrence, Walt Whitman, and Wagner are 'romantic'.

7. Sensibility to natural objects, when solemn and enthusiastic, is 'romantic'. In this sense *The Prelude* is the most 'romantic' poem in the world: and there is much 'romanticism' in Keats, Shelley, de Vigny, de Musset, and Goethe.

It will be seen, of course, that many writers are 'romantic' on more than one account. Thus Morris comes in my first class as well as my second, Mr. Eddison in my second as well as my third, Rousseau in my sixth as well as my fifth, Shelley in my sixth and fifth, and so on. This may suggest some common root, whether historical or psychological, for all seven: but the real qualitative difference between them is shown by the fact that a liking for any one does not imply liking for the others. Though people who are 'romantic' in different senses may turn to the same books, they turn to them for different reasons, and one half of William Morris's readers do not know how the other half live. It makes all the difference in the world whether you like Shelley because he provides a mythology or because he promises a revolution. Thus I myself always loved the second kind of Romanticism and detested the fourth and fifth kinds; I liked the first very little and the third only after I was grown-up—as an acquired taste.

But what I meant by 'Romanticism' when I wrote the *Pilgrim's Regress*—and what I would still be taken to mean on the title page of this book—was not exactly any one of these seven things. What I meant was a particular recurrent experience which dominated my childhood and adolescence and which I hastily called 'Romantic' because inanimate nature and marvellous literature were among the things that evoked it. I still believe that the experience is common, commonly misunderstood, and of immense importance: but I know now that in other minds it arises under other *stimuli* and is entangled with other irrelevancies and that to bring it into the forefront of consciousness is not so easy as I once supposed. I will now try to describe it sufficiently to make the following pages intelligible.

The experience is one of intense longing. It is distinguished from other longings by two things. In the first place, though the sense of want is acute and even painful, yet the mere wanting is felt to be somehow a delight. Other desires are felt as pleasures only if satisfaction is expected in the near future: hunger is pleasant only while we know (or believe) that we are soon going to eat. But this desire, even when there is no hope of possible satisfaction, continues to be prized, and even to be preferred to anything else in the world, by those who have once felt it. This hunger is better than any other fullness; this poverty better than all other wealth. And thus it comes about, that if the desire is long absent, it may itself be desired, and that new desiring becomes a new

7

instance of the original desire, though the subject may not at once recognise the fact and thus cries out for his lost youth of soul at the very moment in which he is being rejuvenated. This sounds complicated, but it is simple when we live it. 'Oh to feel as I did then!' we cry; not noticing that even while we say the words the very feeling whose loss we lament is rising again in all its old bitter-sweetness. For this sweet Desire cuts across our ordinary distinctions between wanting and having. To have it is, by definition, a want: to want it, we find, is to have it.

In the second place, there is a peculiar mystery about the *object* of this Desire. Inexperienced people (and inattention leaves some inexperienced all their lives) suppose, when they feel it, that they know what they are desiring. Thus if it comes to a child while he is looking at a far off hillside he at once thinks 'if only I were there'; if it comes when he is remembering some event in the past, he thinks 'if only I could go back to those days'. If it comes (a little later) while he is reading a 'romantic' tale or poem of 'perilous seas and faerie lands forlorn', he thinks he is wishing that such places really existed and that he could reach them. If it comes (later still) in a context with erotic suggestions he believes he is desiring the perfect beloved. If he falls upon literature (like Maeterlinck or the early Yeats) which treats of spirits and the like with some show of serious belief, he may think that he is hankering for real magic and occultism. When it darts out upon him from his studies in history or science, he may confuse it with the intellectual craving for knowledge.

But every one of these impressions is wrong. The sole merit I claim for this book is that it is written by one who has proved them all to be wrong. There is no room for vanity in the claim: I know them to be wrong not by intelligence but by experience, such experience as would not have come my way if my youth had been wiser, more virtuous, and less self-centred than it was. For I have myself been deluded by every one of these false answers in turn, and have contemplated each of them earnestly enough to discover the cheat. To have embraced so many false Florimels is no matter for boasting: it is fools, they say, who learn by experience. But since they do at last learn, let a fool bring his experience into the common stock that wiser men may profit by it.

Every one of these supposed *objects* for the Desire is inadequate to it.
An easy experiment will show that by going to the far hillside you will
get either nothing, or else a recurrence of the same desire which sent
you thither. A rather more difficult, but still possible, study of your
own memories, will prove that by returning to the past you could not
find, as a possession, that ecstasy which some sudden reminder of the
past now moves you to desire. Those remembered moments were
either quite commonplace at the time (and owe all their enchantment
to memory) or else were themselves moments of desiring. The same is
true of the things described in the poets and marvellous romancers.
The moment we endeavour to think out seriously what it would be like
if they were actual, we discover this. When Sir Arthur Conan Doyle
claimed to have photographed a fairy, I did not, in fact, believe it: but
the mere making of the claim—the approach of the fairy to within even
that hailing distance of actuality—revealed to me at once that if the
claim had succeeded it would have chilled rather than satisfied the
desire which fairy literature had hitherto aroused. Once grant your
fairy, your enchanted forest, your satyr, faun, wood-nymph and well of
immortality *real*, and amidst all the scientific, social and practical
interest which the discovery would awake, the Sweet Desire would
have disappeared, would have shifted its ground, like the cuckoo's
voice or the rainbow's end, and be now calling us from beyond a
further hill. With Magic in the darker sense (as it has been and is
actually practised) we should fare even worse. How if one had gone
that way—had actually called for something and it had come? What
would one feel? Terror, pride, guilt, tingling excitement . . . but what
would all that have to do with our Sweet Desire? It is not at Black
Mass or *séance* that the Blue Flower grows. As for the sexual answer,
that I suppose to be the most obviously false Florimel of all. On whatever plane you take it, it is not what we were looking for. Lust can
be gratified. Another personality can become to us 'our America,
our New-found-land'. A happy marriage can be achieved. But
what has any of the three, or any mixture of the three, to do with that
unnameable something, desire for which pierces us like a rapier at
the smell of a bonfire, the sound of wild ducks flying overhead,
the title of *The Well at the World's End*, the opening lines of *Kubla*

Khan, the morning cobwebs in late summer, or the noise of falling waves?

· It appeared to me therefore that if a man diligently followed this desire, pursuing the false objects until their falsity appeared and then resolutely abandoning them, he must come out at last into the clear knowledge that the human soul was made to enjoy some object that is never fully given—nay, cannot even be imagined as given—in our present mode of subjective and spatio-temporal experience. This Desire was, in the soul, as the Siege Perilous in Arthur's castle—the chair in which only one could sit. And if nature makes nothing in vain, the One who can sit in this chair must exist. I knew only too well how easily the longing accepts false objects and through what dark ways the pursuit of them leads us: but I also saw that the Desire itself contains the corrective of all these errors. The only fatal error was to pretend that you had passed from desire to fruition, when, in reality, you had found either nothing, or desire itself, or the satisfaction of some different desire. The dialectic of Desire, faithfully followed, would retrieve all mistakes, head you off from all false paths, and force you not to propound, but to live through, a sort of ontological proof. This lived dialectic, and the merely argued dialectic of my philosophical progress, seemed to have converged on one goal; accordingly I tried to put them both into my allegory which thus became a defence of Romanticism (in my peculiar sense) as well as of Reason and Christianity.

After this explanation the reader will more easily understand (I do not ask him to condone) the bitterness of certain pages in this book. He will realise how the Post-War period must have looked to one who had followed such a road as mine. The different intellectual move-ments of that time were hostile to one another; but the one thing that seemed to unite them all was their common enmity to 'immortal longings'. The direct attack carried out on them from below by those who followed Freud or D. H. Lawrence, I think I could have borne with some temper; what put me out of patience was the scorn which claimed to be from above, and which was voiced by the American 'Humanists', the Neo-Scholastics, and some who wrote for *The Criterion.* These people seemed to me to be condemning what they did not understand. When they called Romanticism 'nostalgia' I, who had rejected long ago the illusion that the desired object was in the past, felt that they had not even crossed the *Pons Asinorum*. In the end I lost my temper.

If I were now writing a book I could bring the question between those thinkers and myself to a much finer point. One of them described Romanticism as 'spilled religion'. I accept the description. And I agree that he who has religion ought not to spill it. But does it follow that he who finds it spilled should avert his eyes? How if there is a man to whom those bright drops on the floor are the beginning of a trail which, duly followed, will lead him in the end to taste the cup itself? How if no other trail, humanly speaking, were possible? Seen in this light my ten years' old quarrel both with the counter-Romantics on the one hand and with the sub-Romantics on the other (the apostles of instinct and even of gibberish) assumes, I trust, a certain permanent interest. Out of this double quarrel came the dominant image of my allegory—the barren, aching rocks of its 'North', the foetid swamps of its 'South', and between them the Road on which alone mankind can safely walk.

The things I have symbolised by North and South, which are to me equal and opposite evils, each continually strengthened and made plausible by its critique of the other, enter our experience on many different levels. In agriculture we have to fear both the barren soil and the soil which is irresistibly fertile. In the animal kingdom, the crustacean and the jellyfish represent two low solutions of the problem of existence. In our eating, the palate revolts both from excessive bitter and excessive sweet. In art, we find on the one hand, purists and doctrinaires, who would rather (like Scaliger) lose a hundred beauties than admit a single fault, and who cannot believe anything to be good if the unlearned spontaneously enjoy it: on the other hand, we find the uncritical and slovenly artists who will spoil the whole work rather than deny themselves any indulgence of sentiment or humour or sensationalism. Everyone can pick out among his own acquaintance the Northern and Southern types—the high noses, compressed lips, pale complexions, dryness and taciturnity of the one, the open mouths, the facile laughter and tears, the garrulity and (so to speak) general greasiness of the others. The Northerners are the men of rigid systems whether sceptical or dogmatic, Aristocrats, Stoics, Pharisees, Rigorists, signed and sealed members of highly organised 'Parties'. The South-erners are by their very nature less definable; boneless souls whose doors stand open day and ·night to almost every visitant, but always with readiest welcome for those, whether Maenad or Mystagogue, who offer some sort of intoxication. The delicious tang of the forbidden and the unknown draws them on with fatal attraction; the smudging of all frontiers, the relaxation of all resistances, dream, opium, darkness, death, and the return to the womb. Every feeling is justified by the mere fact that it is felt: for a Northerner, every feeling on the same ground is suspect. An arrogant and hasty selectiveness on some narrow *a priori* basis cuts him off from the sources of life. In Theology also there is a North and South. The one cries 'Drive out the bondmaid's son,' and the other 'Quench not the smoking flax'. The one exag-gerates the distinctness between Grace and Nature into a sheer opposi-tion and by vilifying the higher levels of Nature (the real *praeparatio evangelica* inherent in certain immediately sub-Christian experiences) makes the way hard for those who are at the point of coming in. The other blurs the distinction altogether, flatters mere kindliness into thinking it is charity and vague optimisms or pantheisms into thinking that they are Faith, and makes the way out fatally easy and impercep-tible for the budding apostate. The two extremes do not coincide with Romanism (to the North) and Protestantism (to the South). Barth might well have been placed among my Pale Men, and Erasmus might have found himself at home with Mr. Broad.

I take our own age to be predominantly Northern—it is two great 'Northern' powers that are tearing·each other to pieces on the Don while I write. But the matter is complicated, for the rigid and ruthless system of the Nazis has 'Southern' and swamp-like elements at its centre; and when our age is 'Southern' at all, it is excessively so. D. H. Lawrence and the Surrealists have perhaps reached a point further 'South' than humanity ever reached before. And this is what one would expect. Opposite evils, far from balancing, aggravate each other. 'The heresies that men leave are hated most'; widespread drunkenness is the father of Prohibition and Prohibition of widespread drunken-ness. Nature, outraged by one extreme, avenges herself by flying to the other. One can even meet adult males who are not ashamed to attribute their own philosophy to 'Reaction' and do not think the philosophy thereby discredited.

With both the 'North' and the 'South' a man has, I take it, only one concern—to avoid them and hold the Main Road. We must not 'hearken to the over-wise *or* to the over-foolish giant'. We were made to be neither cerebral men nor visceral men, but Men. Not beasts nor angels but Men—things at once rational and animal.

The fact that, if I say anything in explanation of my North and South, I have to say so much, serves to underline a rather important truth about symbols. In the present edition I have tried to make the book easier by a running headline. But I do so with great reluctance. To supply a 'key' to an allegory may encourage that particular misunderstanding of allegory which, as a literary critic, I have elsewhere denounced. It may encourage people to suppose that allegory is a disguise, a way of saying obscurely what could have been said more clearly. But in fact all good allegory exists not to hide but to reveal; to make the inner world more palpable by giving it an (imagined) concrete embodiment. My headline is there only because my allegory failed—partly through my own fault (I am now heartily ashamed of the preposterous allegorical filigree on p. 98), and partly because modern readers are unfamiliar with the method. But it remains true that wherever the symbols are best, the key is least adequate. For when allegory is at its best, it approaches myth, which must be grasped with the imagination, not with the intellect. If, as I still sometimes hope, my North and South and my Mr. Sensible have some touch of mythical life, then no amount of 'explanation' will quite catch up with their meaning. It is the sort of thing you cannot learn from definition: you must rather get to know it as you get to know a smell or a taste, the 'atmosphere' of a family or a country town, or the personality of an individual.

Three other cautions remain to be given. 1. The map on the end leaves has puzzled some readers because, as they say, 'it marks all sorts of places not mentioned in the text'. But so do all maps in travel books. John's route is marked with a dotted line: those who are not interested in the places off that route need not bother about them. They are a half whimsical attempt to fill in the 'Northern' and 'Southern' halves of the world with the spiritual phenomena appropriate to them. Most of the names explain themselves. *Wanhope* is Middle English for Despair; *Woodey* and *Lyssanesos* mean 'Isle of Insanity'; *Behmenheim* is named, unfairly, after Jakob Boehme or Behmen; *Golnesshire* (Anglo-Saxon *Gál*) is the county of Lechery; in *Trine*-land one feels 'in tune with the infinite'; and *Zeitgeistheim*, of course, is the habitat of the *Zeitgeist* or Spirit of the Age. *Naughtstow* is 'a place that is no good at all'. The two military railways were meant to symbolise the double attack from Hell on the two sides of our nature. It was hoped that the roads spreading out from each of the enemy railheads would look rather like claws or tentacles reaching out into the country of Man's Soul. If you like to put little black arrows pointing South on the seven Northern roads (in the fashion of the newspaper war maps) and others pointing North on the six Southern roads, you would get a clear picture of the Holy War as I see it. You might amuse yourself by deciding where to put them— a question that admits different answers. On the Northern front, for example, I should represent the enemy in occupation of Cruelsland and Superbia, and thus threatening the Pale Men with a pincer movement. But I don't claim to know; and doubtless the position shifts every day. 2. The name *Mother Kirk* was chosen because 'Christianity' is not a very convincing name. Its defect was that it not unnaturally led the reader to attribute to me a much more definite *Ecclesiastical* position than I could really boast of. The book is concerned solely with Christianity as against unbelief. 'Denominational' questions do not come in. 3. In this preface the autobiographical element in John has had to be stressed because the source of the obscurities lay there. But you must not assume that everything in the book is autobiographical. I was attempting to generalise, not to tell people about my own life.

C. S. LEWIS

CONTENTS

BOOK ONE
THE DATA

BOOK TWO
THRILL

BOOK THREE
THROUGH DARKEST ZEITGEISTHEIM

Contents

Contents

Contents

BOOK NINE

ACROSS THE CANYON

BOOK TEN

THE REGRESS

THE DATA

This every soul seeketh and for the sake of this doth all her actions, having an inkling that it is; but what it is she cannot sufficiently discern, and she knoweth not her way, and concerning this she hath no constant assurance as she hath of other things.—PLATO

Whose souls, albeit in a cloudy memory, yet seek back their good, but, like drunk men, know not the road home.—BOETHIUS

Somewhat it seeketh, and what that is directly it knoweth not, yet very intentive desire thereof doth so incite it, that all other known delights and pleasures are laid aside, they give place to the search of this but only suspected desire.—HOOKER

Knowledge of broken law precedes all other religious experience

CHAPTER ONE

The Rules

I DREAMED of a boy who was born in the land of Puritania and his name was John. And I dreamed that when John was able to walk he ran out of his parents' garden on a fine morning on to the road. And on the other side of the road there was a deep wood, but not thick, full of primroses and soft green moss. When John set eyes on this he thought he had never seen anything so beautiful: and he ran across the road and into the wood, and was just about to go down on his hands and knees and to pull up the primroses by handfuls, when his mother came running out of the garden gate, and she also ran across the road, and caught John up, and smacked him soundly and told him he must never go into the wood again. And John cried, but he asked no questions, for he was not yet at the age for asking questions. Then a year went past. And then, another fine morning, John had a little sling and he went out into the garden and he saw a bird sitting on a branch. And John got his sling ready and was going to have a shot at the bird, when the cook came running out of the garden and caught John up and smacked him soundly and told him he must never kill any of the birds in the garden.

'Why?' said John.

'Because the Steward would be very angry.' said cook.

'Who is the Steward?' said John.

'He is the man who makes rules for all the country round here,' said cook.

'Why?' said John.

'Because the Landlord set him to do it.'

'Who is the Landlord?' said John.

'He owns all the country,' said the cook.

'Why?' said John.

And when he asked this, the cook went and told his mother. And

20

his mother sat down and talked to John about the Landlord all afternoon: but John took none of it in, for he was not yet at the age for
taking it in. Then a year went past, and one dark, cold, wet morning
John was made to put on new clothes. They were the ugliest clothes
that had ever been put upon him, which John did not mind at all, but
they also caught him under the chin, and were tight under the arms,
which he minded a great deal, and they made him itch all over. And
his father and mother took him out along the road, one holding him
by each hand (which was uncomfortable, too, and very unnecessary),
and told him they were taking him to see the Steward. The Steward
lived in a big dark house of stone on the side of the road. The father
and mother went in to talk to the Steward first, and John was left
sitting in the hall on a chair so high that his feet did not reach the floor.
There were other chairs in the hall where he could have sat in comfort,
but his father had told him that the Steward would be very angry if he
did not sit absolutely still and be very good: and John was beginning
to be afraid, so he sat still in the high chair with his feet dangling, and
his clothes itching all over him, and his eyes starting out of his head.
After a very long time his parents came back again, looking as if they
had been with the doctor, very grave. Then they said that John must
go in and see the Steward too. And when John came into the room,
there was an old man with a red, round face, who was very kind and
full of jokes, so that John quite got over his fears, and they had a good
talk about fishing tackle and bicycles. But just when the talk was at its
best, the Steward got up and cleared his throat. He then took down a
mask from the wall with a long white beard attached to it and suddenly
clapped it on his face, so that his appearance was awful. And he said,
'Now I am going to talk to you about the Landlord. The Landlord
owns all the country, and it is *very, very* kind of him to allow us to live
on it at all—very, very kind.' He went on repeating 'very kind' in a
queer sing-song voice so long that John would have laughed, but that
now he was beginning to be frightened again. The Steward then took
down from a peg a big card with small print all over it, and said,
'Here is a list of all the things the Landlord says you must not do.
You'd better look at it.' So John took the card: but half the rules
seemed to forbid things he had never heard of, and the other half

forbade things he was doing every day and could not imagine not doing: and the number of the rules was so enormous that he felt he could never remember them all. 'I hope,' said the Steward, 'that you have not already broken any of the rules?' John's heart began to thump, and his eyes bulged more and more, and he was at his wit's end when the Steward took the mask off and looked at John with his real face and said, 'Better tell a lie, old chap, better tell a lie. Easiest for all concerned,' and popped the mask on his face all in a flash. John gulped and said quickly, 'Oh, no, sir.' 'That is just as well,' said the Steward through the mask. 'Because, you know, if you did break any of them and the Landlord got to know of it, do you know what he'd do to you?' 'No, sir,' said John: and the Steward's eyes seemed to be twinkling dreadfully through the holes of the mask. 'He'd take you and shut you up for ever and ever in a black hole full of snakes and scorpions as large as lobsters—for ever and ever. And besides that, he is such a kind, good man, so very, very kind, that I am sure you would never *want* to displease him.' 'No, sir,' said John. 'But, please, sir . . .' 'Well,' said the Steward. 'Please, sir, supposing I did break one, one little one, just by accident, you know. Could nothing stop the snakes and lobsters?' 'Ah! . . .' said the Steward; and then he sat down and talked for a long time, but John could not understand a single syllable. However, it all ended with pointing out that the Landlord was quite extraordinarily kind and good to his tenants, and would certainly torture most of them to death the moment he had the slightest pretext. 'And you can't blame him,' said the Steward. 'For after all, it *is* his land, and it is so very good of him to let us live here at all—people like us, you know.' Then the Steward took off the mask and had a nice, sensible chat with John again, and gave him a cake and brought him out to his father and mother. But just as they were going he bent down and whispered in John's ear, 'I shouldn't bother about it all too much if I were you.' At the same time he slipped the card of the rules into John's hand and told him he could keep it for his own use.

CHAPTER TWO

The Island

Now the days and the weeks went on again, and I dreamed that John had little peace either by day or night for thinking of the rules and the black hole full of snakes. At first he tried very hard to keep them all, but when it came to bed-time he always found that he had broken far more than he had kept: and the thought of the horrible tortures to which the good, kind Landlord would put him became such a burden that next day he would become quite reckless and break as many as he possibly could; for oddly enough this eased his mind for the moment. But then after a few days the fear would return and this time it would be worse than before because of the dreadful number of rules that he had broken during the interval. But what puzzled him most at this time was a discovery which he made after the rules had been hanging in his bedroom for two or three nights: namely, that on the other side of the card, on the back, there was quite a different set of rules. There were so many that he never read them all through and he was always finding new ones. Some of them were very like the rules on the front of the card, but most of them were just the opposite. Thus whereas the front of the card said that you must be always examining yourself to see how many rules you had broken, the back of the card began like this:

Rule 1.—Put the whole thing out of your head
     The moment you get into bed.

Or again, whereas the front said that you must always go and ask your elders what the rule about a certain thing was, if you were in the least doubt, the back said:

Rule 2.—Unless they saw you do it,
     Keep quiet or else you'll rue it.

And so on. And now I dreamed that John went out one morning and tried to play in the road and to forget his troubles; but the rules kept

coming back into his head so that he did not make much of it. However, he went on always a few yards further till suddenly he looked up
and saw that he was so far away from home that he was in a part of the
road he had never seen before. Then came the sound of a musical
instrument, from behind it seemed, very sweet and very short, as if it
were one plucking of a string or one note of a bell, and after it a full,
clear voice—and it sounded so high and strange that he thought it was
very far away, further than a star. The voice said, Come. Then John
saw that there was a stone wall beside the road in that part: but it had
(what he had never seen in a garden wall before) a window. There
was no glass in the window and no bars; it was just a square hole in
the wall. Through it he saw a green wood full of primroses: and he
remembered suddenly how he had gone into another wood to pull
primroses, as a child, very long ago—so long that even in the moment
of remembering the memory seemed still out of reach. While he strained
to grasp it, there came to him from beyond the wood a sweetness and a
pang so piercing that instantly he forgot his father's house, and his
mother, and the fear of the Landlord, and the burden of the rules. All
the furniture of his mind was taken away. A moment later he found
that he was sobbing, and the sun had gone in: and what it was that
had happened to him he could not quite remember, nor whether it had
happened in this wood, or in the other wood when he was a child. It
seemed to him that a mist which hung at the far end of the wood had
parted for a moment, and through the rift he had seen a calm sea, and
in the sea an island, where the smooth turf sloped down unbroken to
the bays, and out of the thickets peeped the pale, small-breasted Oreads,
wise like gods, unconscious of themselves like beasts, and tall enchan-
ters, bearded to their feet, sat in green chairs among the forests. But even
while he pictured these things he knew, with one part of his mind,
that they were not like the things he had seen—nay, that what had
befallen him was not seeing at all. But he was too young to heed the
distinction: and too empty, now that the unbounded sweetness passed
away, not to seize greedily whatever it had left behind. He had no
inclination yet to go into the wood: and presently he went home, with
a sad excitement upon him, repeating to himself a thousand times, 'I
know now what I want.' The first time that he said it, he was aware

that it was not entirely true: but before he went to bed he was believing it.

CHAPTER THREE

The Eastern Mountains

JOHN had a disreputable old uncle who was the tenant of a poor little farm beside his father's. One day when John came in from the garden, he found a great hubbub in the house. His uncle was sitting there with his cheeks the colour of ashes. His mother was crying. His father was sitting very still with a solemn face. And there, in the midst of them, was the Steward with his mask on. John crept round to his mother and asked her what the matter was.

'Poor Uncle George has had notice to quit,' she said.

'Why?' said John.

'His lease is up. The Landlord has sent him notice to quit.'

'But didn't you know how long the lease was for?'

'Oh, no, indeed we did not. We thought it was for years and years more. I am sure the Landlord never gave us any idea he was going to turn him out at a moment's notice like this.'

'Ah, but it doesn't need any notice,' broke in the Steward, 'You know he always retains the right to turn anyone out whenever he chooses. It is very good of him to let any of us stay here at all.'

'To be sure, to be sure,' said the mother.

'That goes without saying,' said the father.

'I'm not complaining,' said Uncle George. 'But it seems cruelly hard.'

'Not at all,' said the Steward. 'You've only got to go to the Castle and knock at the gate and see the Landlord himself. You know that he's only turning you out of here to make you much more comfortable somewhere else. Don't you?'

Uncle George nodded. He did not seem able to get his voice.

Suddenly the father looked at his watch. Then he looked up at the Steward and said:

An uncomfortable funeral, lacking both Pagan fortitude and Christian hope

'Well?'

'Yes,' said the Steward.

Then John was sent up to his bedroom and told to put on the ugly and uncomfortable clothes; and when he came downstairs, itching all over, and tight under the arms, he was given a little mask to put on, and his parents put masks on too. Then I thought in my dream that they wanted to put a mask on Uncle George, but he was trembling so that it would not stay on. So they had to see his face as it was; and his face became so dreadful that everyone looked in a different direction and pretended not to see it. They got Uncle George to his feet with much difficulty, and then they all came out on to the road. The sun was just setting at one end of the road, for the road ran east and west. They turned their backs on the dazzling western sky and there John saw ahead of them the night coming down over the eastern mountains. The country sloped down eastward to a brook, and all this side of the brook was green and cultivated: on the other side of the brook a great black moor sloped upward, and beyond that were the crags and chasms of the lower mountains, and high above them again the bigger moun-tains: and on top of the whole waste was one mountain so big and black that John was afraid of it. He was told that the Landlord had his castle up there.

They trudged on eastward, a long time, always descending, till they came to the brook. They were so low now that the sunset behind them was out of sight. Before them, all was growing darker every minute, and the cold east wind was blowing out of the darkness, right from the mountain tops. When they had stood for a little, Uncle George looked round on them all once or twice, and said, 'Oh, dear! Oh, dear!' in a funny small voice like a child's. Then he stepped over the brook and began to walk away up the moor. It was now so dark and there were so many ups and downs in the moorland that they lost sight of him almost at once. Nobody ever saw him again.

'Well,' said the Steward, untying his mask as they turned home-ward. 'We've all got to go when our time comes.'

'That's true,' said the father, who was lighting his pipe. When it was lit he turned to the Steward and said: 'Some of those pigs of George's have won prizes.'

'I'd keep 'em if I were you,' said the Steward. 'It's no time for selling now.'

'Perhaps you're right,' said the father.

John walked behind with his mother.

'Mother.'

'Well, dear?'

'Could any of us be turned out without notice like that any day?'

'Well, yes. But it is very unlikely.'

'But we *might* be?'

'You oughtn't to be thinking of that sort of thing at your age.'

'Why oughtn't I?'

'It's not healthy. A boy like you.'

'Mother.'

'Yes?'

'Can *we* break off the lease without notice too?'

'How do you mean?'

'Well, the Landlord can turn us out of the farm whenever he likes. Can we leave the farm whenever we like?'

'No, certainly not.'

' Why not?'

'That's in the lease. We must go when he likes, and stay as long as he likes.'

'Why?'

'I suppose because he makes the leases.'

'What would happen if we did leave?'

'He would be very angry.'

'Would he put us in the black hole?'

'Perhaps.'

'Mother.'

'Well, dear?'

'Will the Landlord put Uncle George in the black hole?'

'How dare you say such a thing about your poor uncle? Of course he won't.'

'But hasn't Uncle George broken all the rules?'

'Broken all the rules? Your Uncle George was a very good man.'

'You never told me that before,' said John.

27

CHAPTER FOUR

Leah for Rachel

THEN I turned over in my sleep and began to dream deeper still: and I dreamed that I saw John growing tall and lank till he ceased to be a child and became a boy. The chief pleasure of his life in these days was to go down the road and look through the window in the wall in the hope of seeing the beautiful Island. Some days he saw it well enough, especially at first, and heard the music and the voice. At first he would not look through the window into the wood unless he had heard the music. But after a time both the sight of the Island, and the sounds, became very rare. He would stand looking through the window for hours, and seeing the wood, but no sea or Island beyond it, and straining his ears but hearing nothing except the wind in the leaves. And the yearning for that sight of the Island and the sweet wind blowing over the water from it, though indeed these themselves had given him only yearning, became so terrible that John thought he would die if he did not have them again soon. He even said to himself, 'I would break every rule on the card for them if I could only get them. I would go down into the black hole for ever if it had a window from which I could see the island.' Then it came into his head that perhaps he ought to explore the wood and thus he might find his way down to the sea beyond it: so he determined that the next day, whatever he saw or heard at the window, he would go through and spend the whole day in the wood. When the morning came, it had been raining all night and a south wind had blown the clouds away at sunrise, and all was fresh and shining. As soon as he had had his breakfast John was out on the road. With the wind and the birds, and country carts passing, there were many noises about that morning, so that when John heard a strain of music long before he had reached the wall and the window —a strain like that which he desired, but coming from an unexpected quarter—he could not be absolutely certain that he had not imagined it. It made him stand still in the road for a minute, and in my dream I could hear him thinking—like this: 'If I go after that sound—away off

28

the road, up yonder—it is all luck whether I shall find anything at all.
But if I go on to the window, there I *know* I shall reach the wood, and
there I can have a good hunt for the shore and the Island. In fact, I
shall *insist* on finding it. I am determined to. But if I go a new way I
shall not be able to insist: I shall just have to take what comes.' So he
went on to the place he knew and climbed through the window into
the wood. Up and down and to and fro among the trees he walked,
looking this way and that: but he found no sea and no shore, and
indeed no end to the wood in any direction. When it came to the
middle of the day he was so hot that he sat down and fanned himself.
Often, of late, when the sight of the Island had been withheld, he had
felt sad and despairing: but what he felt now was more like anger. 'I
must have it.' he kept on saying to himself, and then, 'I must have
something.' Then it occurred to him that at least he had the wood,
which he would once have loved, and that he had not given it a
thought all morning. Very well, thought John, I will enjoy the wood:
I *will* enjoy it. He set his teeth and wrinkled his forehead and sat still
until the sweat rolled off him in an effort to enjoy the wood. But the
more he tried the more he felt that there was nothing to enjoy. There
was the grass and there were the trees: 'But what am I to *do* with them?'
said John. Next it came into his head that he might perhaps get the old
feeling—for what, he thought, had the Island ever given him but a
feeling?—by imagining. He shut his eyes and set his teeth again and
made a picture of the Island in his mind: but he could not keep his
attention on the picture because he wanted all the time to watch some
other part of his mind to see if the *feeling* were beginning. But no feeling
began: and then, just as he was opening his eyes he heard a voice
speaking to him. It was quite close at hand, and very sweet, and not at
all like the old voice of the wood. When he looked round he saw what
he had never expected, yet he was not surprised. There in the grass
beside him sat a laughing brown girl of about his own age, and she
had no clothes on.

'It was me you wanted,' said the brown girl. 'I am better than your
silly Islands.'

And John rose and caught her, all in haste, and committed fornica-
tion with her in the wood.

29

CHAPTER FIVE

Ichabod

AFTER that John was always going to the wood. He did not always have his pleasure of her in the body, though it often ended that way: sometimes he would talk to her about himself, telling her lies about his courage and his cleverness. All that he told her she remembered, so that on other days she could tell it over to him again. Sometimes, even, he would go with her through the wood looking for the sea and the Island, but not often. Meanwhile the year went on and the leaves began to fall in the wood and the skies were more often grey: until now, as I dreamed, John had slept in the wood, and he woke up in the wood. The sun was low and a blustering wind was stripping the leaves from the branches. The girl was still there and the appearance of her was hateful to John: and he saw that she knew this, and the more she knew it the more she stared at him, smiling. He looked round and saw how small the wood was after all—a beggarly strip of trees between the road and a field that he knew well. Nowhere in sight was there anything that he liked at all.

'I shall not come back here,' said John. 'What I wanted is not here. It wasn't you I wanted, you know.'

'Wasn't it?' said the brown girl. 'Then be off. But you must take your family with you.'

With that she put up her hands to her mouth and called. Instantly from behind every tree there slipped out a brown girl: each of them was just like herself: the little wood was full of them.

'What are these?'

'Our daughters,' said she. 'Did you not know you were a father? Did you think I was barren, you fool? And now, children,' she added, turning to the mob, 'go with your father.'

Suddenly John became very much afraid and leaped over the wall into the road. There he ran home as fast as he could.

30

CHAPTER SIX

Quem Quaeritis in Sepulchro? Non est Hic

FROM that day forth until he left his home John was not happy. First of all the weight of all the rules that he had broken descended upon him: for while he was going daily to the wood he had almost forgotten the Landlord, and now suddenly the whole reckoning was to pay. In the second place, his last sight of the Island was now so long ago that he had forgotten how to wish for it even, and almost how to set about looking for it. At first he feared to go back to the window in the wall, lest he should meet the brown girl: but he soon found that her family were so constantly with him that place made no difference. Wherever he sat down to rest on a walk, there sooner or later, there would be a little brown girl beside him. When he sat of an evening with his father and mother, a brown girl, visible only to him, would sidle in and sit at his feet: and sometimes his mother would fix her eyes on him and even ask him what he was staring at. But most of all they plagued him whenever he had a fit of fright about the Landlord and the black hole. It was always the same. He would wake one morning full of fear, and take down his card and read it—the front of it—and determine that today he would really begin to keep the rules. And for that day he would, but the strain was intolerable. He used to comfort himself by saying, It will get more easy as I go on. To-morrow it will be easier. But to-morrow was always harder, and on the third day it was worst of all. And on that third day when he crept away to bed, tired to death and raw in his soul, always he would be sure to find a brown girl waiting for him there: and on such a night he had no spirit to resist her blandishments.

But when he perceived that no place was more, or less, haunted than another, then he came sidling back to the window in the wall. He had little hopes of it. He visited it more as a man visits a grave. It was full winter now, and the grove was naked and dark, the trees dripped in it, and the stream—he saw now that it was little more than a gutter—was full of dead leaves and mud. The wall, too, was broken where he had jumped over it. Yet John stood there a long time, many a winter evening, looking in. And he seemed to himself to have reached the bottom of misery.

One night he was trudging home from it, when he began to weep. He thought of that first day when he had heard the music and seen the Island: and the longing, not now for the Island itself, but for that moment when he had so sweetly longed for it, began to swell up in a warm wave, sweeter, sweeter, till he thought he could bear no more, and then yet sweeter again, till on the top of it, unmistakably, there came the short sound of music, as if a string had been plucked or a bell struck once. At the same moment a coach had gone past him. He turned and looked after it, in time to see a head even then being withdrawn from the window: and he thought he heard a voice say, Come. And far beyond the coach, among the hills of the western horizon, he thought that he saw a shining sea. and a faint shape of an Island, not much more than a cloud. It was nothing compared with what he had seen the first time: it was so much further away. But his mind was made up. That night he waited till his parents were asleep, and then, putting some few needments together, he stole out by the back door and set his face to the West to seek for the Island.

BOOK TWO

THRILL

Thou shalt not make to thyself any graven image, nor the likeness of anything that is in the heaven above.—EXODUS

The soul of man, therefore, desiring to learn what manner of things these are, casteth her eyes upon objects akin to herself, whereof none sufficeth. And then it is that she saith, With the Lord and with the things whereof I spoke, there is nothing in that likeness; what then is it like? This is the question, oh son of Dionysius, that is the cause of all evils—or rather the travail wherein the soul travaileth about it.—PLATO [1]

> *Following false copies of the good, that no*
> *Sincere fulfilment of their promise make.*—DANTE

> *In hand she boldly took*
> *To make another like the former dame,*
> *Another Florimell in shape and look*
> *So lively and so like that many it mistook.*—SPENSER

[1] Some think it wrongly attributed to him.

B   L.P.R.

CHAPTER ONE

Dixit Insipiens

STILL I lay dreaming in bed, and looked, and I saw John go plodding along the road westward in the bitter black of a frosty night. He walked so long that the morning broke. Then presently John saw a little inn by the side of the road and a woman with a broom who had opened the door and was sweeping out the rubbish. So he turned in there and called for a breakfast, and while it was cooking he sat down in a hard chair by the newly-lit fire and fell asleep. When he woke the sun was shining in through the window and there was his breakfast laid. Another traveller was already eating: he was a big man with red hair and a red stubble on all his three chins, buttoned up very tight. When they had both finished the traveller rose and cleared his throat and stood with his back to the fire. Then he cleared his throat again and said:

'A fine morning, young sir.'

'Yes, sir,' said John.

'You are going West, perhaps, young man?'

'I—I think so.'

'It is possible that you don't know me.'

'I am a stranger here.'

'No offence,' said the stranger. 'My name is Mr. Enlightenment, and I believe it is pretty generally known. I shall be happy to give you my assistance and protection as far as our ways lie together.'

John thanked him very much for this and when they went out from the inn there was a neat little trap waiting, with a fat little pony between the shafts: and its eyes were so bright and its harness was so well polished that it was difficult to say which was twinkling the keener in the morning sunshine. They both got into the trap and Mr. Enlighten-ment whipped up the fat little pony and they went bowling along the road as if nobody had a care in the world. Presently they began to talk.

'And where might you come from, my fine lad?' said Mr. Enlight-enment.

'From Puritania, sir,' said John.

'A good place to leave, eh?' ·

'I am so glad you think that,' cried John. 'I was afraid——'

'I hope I am a man of the world,' said Mr. Enlightenment. 'Any young fellow who is anxious to better himself may depend on finding sympathy and support in me. Puritania! Why, I suppose you have been brought up to be afraid of the Landlord.'— God ·

'Well, I must admit I sometimes *do* feel rather nervous.'

'You may make your mind easy, my boy. There is no such person.'

'There is no Landlord?'

'There is absolutely no such thing—I might even say no such *entity* —in existence. There never has been and never will be.'

'And is this absolutely certain?' cried John; for a great hope was rising in his heart.

'Absolutely certain. Look at me, young man. I ask you—do I look as if I was easily taken in?'

'Oh, no,' said John hastily. 'I was just wondering, though. I mean —how did they all come to think there was such a person?'

'The Landlord is an invention of those Stewards. All made up to keep the rest of us under their thumb: and of course the Stewards are hand in glove with the police. They are a shrewd lot, those Stewards. They know which side their bread is buttered on, all right. Clever fellows. Damn me, I can't help admiring them.'

'But do you mean that the Stewards don't believe it themselves?'

'I dare say they do. It is just the sort of cock and bull story they would believe. They are simple old souls most of them—just like children. They have no knowledge of modern science and they would believe anything they were told.'

John was silent for a few minutes. Then he began again:

'But how do you *know* there is no Landlord?'

'Christopher Columbus, Galileo, the earth is round, invention of printing, gunpowder! !' exclaimed Mr. Enlightenment in such a loud voice that the pony shied.

'I beg your pardon,' said John.

'Eh?' said Mr. Enlightenment.

'I didn't quite understand,' said John.

35

'Why, it's as plain as a pikestaff,' said the other. 'Your people in Puritania believe in the Landlord because they have not had the bene-fits of a scientific training. For example, now, I dare say it would be news to you to hear that the earth was round—round as an orange, my lad!'

'Well, I don't know that it would,' said John, feeling a little disap-pointed. 'My father always said it was round.'

'No, no, my dear boy,' said Mr. Enlightenment, 'you must have misunderstood him. It is well known that everyone in Puritania thinks the earth flat. It is not likely that I should be mistaken on such a point. Indeed, it is out of the question. Then again, there is the palæontologi-cal evidence.'

'What's that?'

'Why, they tell you in Puritania that the Landlord made all these roads. But that is quite impossible for old people can remember the time when the roads were not nearly so good as they are now. And what is more, scientists have found all over the country the traces of *old* roads running in quite different directions. The inference is obvious.'

John said nothing.

'I said,' repeated Mr. Enlightenment, 'that the inference was ob-vious.'

'Oh, yes, yes, of course,' said John hastily, turning a little red.

'Then, again, there is anthropology.'

'I'm afraid I don't know——'

'Bless me, of course you don't. They don't mean you to know. An anthropologist is a man who goes round your backward villages in these parts, collecting the odd stories that the country people tell about the Landlord. Why, there is one village where they think he has a trunk like an elephant. Now anyone can see that that couldn't be true.'

'It is very unlikely.'

'And what is better still, we know how the villagers came to think so. It all began by an elephant escaping from the local zoo; and then some old villager—he was probably drunk—saw it wandering about on the mountain one night, and so the story grew up that the Landlord had a trunk.'

'Did they catch the elephant again?'

'Did who?'

'The anthropologists.'

'Oh, my dear boy, you are misunderstanding. This happened long before there were any anthropologists.'

'Then how do they know?'

'Well, as to that . . . I see that you have a very crude notion of how science actually works. To put it simply—for, of course, you could not understand the *technical* explanation—to put it simply, they know that the escaped elephant must have been the source of the trunk story because they know that an escaped snake must have been the source of the snake story in the next village—and so on. This is called the inductive method. Hypothesis, my dear young friend, establishes itself by a cumulative process: or, to use popular language, if you make the same guess often enough it ceases to be a guess and becomes a Scientific Fact.

After he had thought for a while, John said:

'I think I see. Most of the stories about the Landlord are probably untrue; therefore the rest are probably untrue.'

'Well, that is as near as a beginner can get to it, perhaps. But when you have had a scientific training you will find that you can be quite certain about all sorts of things which now seem to you only probable.'

By this time the fat little pony had carried them several miles, and they had come to a place where a by-road went off to the right. 'If you are going West, we must part here,' said Mr. Enlightenment, drawing up. 'Unless perhaps you would care to come home with me. You see that magnificent city?' John looked down by the by-road and saw in a flat plain without any trees a huge collection of corrugated iron huts, most of which seemed rather old and rusty.

'That,' said Mr. Enlightenment, 'is the city of Claptrap. You will hardly believe me when I say that I can remember it as a miserable village. When I first came here it had only forty inhabitants: it now boasts a population of twelve million, four hundred thousand, three hundred and sixty-one souls, who include, I may add, the majority of our most influential publicists and scientific popularizers. In this unprecedented development I am proud to say that I have borne no small part: but it is no mock modesty to add that the invention of the printing press has been more important than any merely personal agency. If you would care to join us——'

'Well, thank you,' said John, 'but I think I will keep to the main road a little longer.'

He got out of the trap and turned to bid good-bye to Mr. Enlighten- ment. Then a sudden thought came into his head, and he said:

'I am not sure that I have really understood all your arguments, sir. Is it absolutely certain that there is no Landlord?'

'Absolutely. I give you my word of honour.'

With these words they shook hands. Mr. Enlightenment turned the pony's head up the by-road, gave it a touch with the whip, and in a few moments was out of sight.

CHAPTER TWO

The Hill

THEN I saw John bounding forward on his road so lightly that before he knew it he had come to the top of a little hill. It was not because the hill had tired him that he stopped there, but because he was too happy to move. 'There is no Landlord,' he cried. Such a weight had been lifted from his mind that he felt he could fly. All round him the frost was gleaming like silver; the sky was like blue glass; a robin sat in the hedge beside him: a cock was crowing in the distance. 'There is no Landlord.' He laughed when he thought of the old card of rules hung over his bed in the bedroom, so low and dark, in his father's house. 'There is no Landlord. There is no black hole.' He turned and looked back on the road he had come by: and when he did so he gasped with joy. For there in the East, under the morning light, he saw the moun- tains heaped up to the sky like clouds, green and violet and dark red; shadows were passing over the big rounded slopes, and water shone in the mountain pools, and up at the highest of all the sun was smiling steadily on the ultimate crags. These crags were indeed so shaped that you could easily take them for a castle: and now it came into John's head that he had never looked at the mountains before, because, as long as he thought that the Landlord lived there, he had been afraid of them. But now that there was no Landlord he perceived that they were beautiful. For a moment he almost doubted whether the Island could be more beautiful, and whether he would not be wiser to go East. instead of West. But it did not seem to him to matter, for he said, 'If the world has the mountains at one end and the Island at the other, then every road leads to beauty, and the world is a glory among glories.'

At that moment he saw a man walking up the hill to meet him. Now I knew in my dream that this man's name was Mr. Vertue, and he was about of an age with John, or a little older.

'What is the name of this place?' said John.

'It is called Jehovah-Jirah,' said Mr. Vertue.

Then they both turned and continued their journey to the West. After they had gone a little way Mr. Vertue stole a glance at John's face and then he smiled a little.

'Why do you smile?' said John.

'I was thinking that you looked very glad.'

'So would you be if you had lived in the fear of a Landlord all your life and had just discovered that you were a free man.'

'Oh, it's that, is it?'

'You don't believe in the Landlord, do you?'

'I know nothing about him—except by hearsay like the rest of us.'

'You wouldn't like to be under his thumb.'

'Wouldn't like? I wouldn't *be* under anyone's thumb.'

'You might have to, if he had a black hole.'

'I'd let him put me in the black hole sooner than take orders if the orders were not to my mind.'

'Why, I think you are right. I can hardly believe it yet—that I need not obey the rules. There's that robin again. To think that I could have a shot at it if I liked and no one would interfere with me!'

'Do you want to?'

'I'm not sure that I do,' said John, fingering his sling. But when he looked round on the sunshine and remembered his great happiness and looked twice at the bird, he said, 'No, I don't. There is nothing I want less. Still—I could if I liked.'

'You mean you could if you chose.'

'Where's the difference?'

'All the difference in the world.'

CHAPTER THREE

A Little Southward

I THOUGHT that John would have questioned him further, but now they came in sight of a woman who was walking slower than they so that presently they came up with her and wished her good-day. When she turned, they saw that she was young and comely, though a little dark of complexion. She was friendly and frank, but not wanton like the brown girls, and the whole world became pleasanter to the young men because they were travelling the same way with her. But first they told her their names, and she told them hers, which was Media Half-ways.

'And where are you travelling to, Mr. Vertue?' she asked.

'To travel hopefully is better than to arrive,' said Vertue.

'Do you mean you are just out for a walk, just for exercise?'

'Certainly not,' said Vertue, who was becoming a little confused. 'I am on a pilgrimage. I must admit, now that you press me, I have not a very clear idea of the end. But that is not the important question. These speculations don't make one a better walker. The great thing is to do one's thirty miles a day.'

'Why?'

'Because that is the rule.'

'Ho-ho!' said John. 'So you *do* believe in the Landlord after all.'

'Not at all. I didn't say it was the Landlord's rule.'

'Whose is it then?'

'It is my own rule. I made it myself.'

'But why?'

'Well, that again is a speculative question. I have made the best rules I can. If I find any better ones I shall adopt them. In the meantime, the great thing is to have rules of some sort and to keep them.'

'And where are *you* going?' said Media, turning to John.

Then John began to tell his companions about the Island, and how he had first seen it, and was determined to give up everything for the hope of finding it.

'Then you had better come and see my father,' said she. 'He lives in the city of Thrill, and at the bottom of this hill there is a turn to the left which will bring us there in half an hour.'

'Has your father been to the Island? Does he know the way?'

'He often talks about something very like it.'

'You had better come with us, Vertue,' said John, 'since you do not know where you are going and there can be no place better to go than the Island.'

'Certainly not,' said Vertue. 'We must keep to the road. We must keep on.'

'I don't see why,' said John.

'I dare say you don't,' said Vertue.

All this time they were going down the hill, and now they came to a little grassy lane on the left which went off through a wood. Then I thought that John had a little hesitation: but partly because the sun was now hot and the hard metal of the road was becoming sore to his feet, and partly because he felt a little angry with Vertue, and most of all because Media was going that way, he decided to turn down the lane. They said good-bye to Vertue, and he went on his way stumping up the next hill without ever looking back.

CHAPTER FOUR

Soft Going

WHEN they were in the lane they walked more gently. The grass was soft under their feet, and the afternoon sun beating down on the sheltered place made it warm. And presently they heard a sound of sweet and melancholy chimes.

'Those are the bells of the city,' said Media.

As they went on they walked closer together, and soon they were

41

walking arm in arm. Then they kissed each other: and after that they went on their way kissing and talking in slow voices, of sad and beautiful things. And the shadow of the wood and the sweetness of the girl and the sleepy sound of the bells reminded John a little bit of the Island, and a little bit of the brown girls.

'This is what I have been looking for all my life,' said John. 'The brown girls were too gross and the Island was too fine. This is the real thing.'

'This is Love,' said Media with a deep sigh. 'This is the way to the *real* Island.'

Then I dreamed that they came in sight of the city, very old, and full of spires and turrets, all covered with ivy, where it lay in a little grassy valley, built on both sides of a lazy, winding river. And they passed the gate in the ruinous old city wall and came and knocked at a certain door and were let in. Then Media brought him in to a darkish room with a vaulted roof and windows of stained glass, and exquisite food was brought to them. With the food came old Mr. Halfways. He was a gliding gentleman with soft, silver hair and a soft, silver voice, dressed in flowing robes: and he was so solemn, with his long beard, that John was reminded of the Steward with his mask on. 'But it is much better than the Steward,' thought John, 'because there is nothing to be afraid of. Also, he doesn't need a mask: his face is really like that.'

CHAPTER FIVE

Leah for Rachel

As they ate John told him about the Island.

'You will find your Island here,' said Mr. Halfways, looking into John's eyes.

'But how can it be here in the middle of the city?'

'It needs no place. It is everywhere and nowhere. It refuses entry to none who asks. It is an Island of the Soul,' said the old gentleman. 'Surely even in Puritania they told you that the Landlord's castle was within you?'

'But I don't want the castle,' said John. 'And I don't believe in the Landlord.'

'What is truth?' said the old man. 'They were mistaken when they told you of the Landlord: and yet they were not mistaken. What the imagination seizes as beauty must be truth, whether it existed before or not. The Landlord they dreamed to find, we find in our hearts: the Island you seek for, you already inhabit. The children of that country are never far from their fatherland.'

When the meal was ended the old gentleman took a harp, and at the first sweep of his hand across the strings John began to think of the music that he had heard by the window in the wall. Then came the voice: and it was no longer merely silver sweet and melancholy like Mr. Halfways' speaking voice, but strong and noble and full of strange over-tones, the noise of the sea, and of all birds, and sometimes of wind and thunder. And John began to see a picture of the Island with his eyes open: but it was more than a picture, for he sniffed the spicy smell and the sharp brine of the sea mixed with it. He seemed to be in the water, only a few yards from the sand of the Island. He could see more than he had ever seen before. But just as he had put down his feet and touched a sandy bottom and was beginning to wade ashore, the song ceased. The whole vision went away. John found himself back in the dusky room, seated on a low divan, with Media by his side.

'Now I shall sing you something else,' said Mr. Halfways.

'Oh, no,' cried John, who was sobbing. 'Sing the same again. Please sing it again.'

'You had better not hear it twice in the same evening. I have plenty of other songs.'

'I would die to hear the first one again,' said John.

'Well, well,' said Mr. Halfways, 'perhaps you know best, Indeed, what does it matter? It is as short to the Island one way as another.' Then he smiled indulgently and shook his head, and John could not help thinking that his talking voice and talking manner were almost silly after the singing. But as soon as the great deep wail of the music began again it swept everything else from his mind. It seemed to him that this time he got more pleasure from the first few notes, and even noticed delicious passages which had escaped him at the first hearing;

43

and he said to himself, 'This is going to be even better than the other. I shall keep my head this time and sip all the pleasure at my ease.' I saw that he settled himself more comfortably to listen and Media slipped her hand into his. It pleased him to think that they were going to the Island together. Now came the vision of the Island again: but this time it was changed, for John scarcely noticed the Island because of a lady with a crown on her head who stood waiting for him on the shore. She was fair, divinely fair. 'At last,' said John, 'a girl with no trace of brown.' And he began again to wade ashore holding out his arms to embrace that queen: and his love for her appeared to him so great and so pure, and they had been parted for so long, that his pity for himself and her almost overwhelmed him. And as he was about to embrace her the song stopped.

'Sing it again, sing it again,' cried John, 'I liked it better the second time.'

'Well, if you insist,' said Mr. Halfways with a shrug. 'It is nice to have a really appreciative audience.' So he sang it the third time. This time John noticed yet more about the music. He began to see how several of the effects were produced and that some parts were better than others. He wondered if it were not a trifle too long. The vision of the Island was a little shadowy this time, and he did not take much notice of it. He put his arm round Media and they lay cheek to cheek. He began to wonder if Mr. Halfways would never end: and when at last the final passage closed, with a sobbing break in the singer's voice, the old gentleman looked up and saw how the young people lay in one another's arms. Then he rose and said:

'You have found your Island—you have found it in one another's hearts.'

Then he tiptoed from the room, wiping his eyes.

CHAPTER SIX

Ichabod

'MEDIA, I love you,' said John.

'We have come to the *real* Island,' said Media.

'But oh, alas!' said he, 'so long our bodies why do we forbear?'

'Else a great prince in prison lies,' sighed she.

'No one else can understand the mystery of our love,' said he.

At that moment a brisk, hobnailed step was heard and a tall young man strode into the room carrying a light in his hand. He had coal-black hair and a straight mouth like the slit in a pillar-box, and he was dressed in various kinds of metal wire. As soon as he saw them he burst into a great guffaw. The lovers instantly sprang up and apart.

'Well, Brownie,' said he, 'at your tricks again?'

'Don't call me that name,' said Media, stamping her foot. 'I have told you before not to call me that.'

The young man made an obscene gesture at her, and then turned to John, 'I see that old fool of a father of mine has been at you?'

'You have no right to speak that way of father,' said Media. Then, turning to John, her cheeks flaming, her breast heaving, she said, 'All is over. Our dream—is shattered. Our mystery—is profaned. I would have taught you all the secrets of love, and now you are lost to me for ever. We must part. I shall go and kill myself,' and with that she rushed from the room.

CHAPTER SEVEN

Non est Hic

'DON'T bother about her,' said the young man. 'She has threatened that a hundred times. She is only a brown girl, though she doesn't know it.'

'A brown girl!' cried John. 'And your father . . . '

'My father has been in the pay of the Brownies all his life. He doesn't know it, the old chuckle-head. Calls them the Muses, or the Spirit, or some rot. In actual fact, he is by profession a pimp.'

'And the Island?' said John.

'We'll talk about it in the morning. Ain't the kind of Island you're thinking of. Tell you what. I don't live with my father and my precious sister. I live in Eschropolis and I am going back to-morrow. I'll take you down to the laboratory and show you some *real* poetry. Not fanta-sies. The real thing.'

'Thank you very much,' said John.

Then young Mr. Halfways found his room for him and the whole of that household went to bed.

CHAPTER EIGHT

Great Promises

GUS HALFWAYS was the name of Mr. Halfways' son. As soon as he rose in the morning he called John down to breakfast with him so that they might start on their journey. There was no one to hinder them, for old Halfways was still asleep and Media always had breakfast in bed. When they had eaten, Gus brought him into a shed beside his father's house and showed him a machine on wheels.

'What is this?' said John.

'My old bus,' said young Halfways. Then he stood back with his head on one side and gazed at it for a bit: but presently he began to speak in a changed and reverent voice.

'She is a poem. She is the daughter of the spirit of the age. What was the speed of Atalanta to her speed? The beauty of Apollo to her beauty?'

Now beauty to John meant nothing save glimpses of his Island, and the machine did not remind him of his Island at all: so he held his tongue.

'Don't you see?' said Gus. 'Our fathers made images of what they called gods and goddesses; but they were really only brown girls and brown boys whitewashed—as anyone found out by looking at them too long. All self-deception and phallic sentiment. But here you have the real art. Nothing erotic about *her,* eh?'

'Certainly not,' said John, looking at the cog-wheels and coils of wire, 'it is certainly not at all like a brown girl.' It was, in fact, more like a nest of hedgehogs and serpents.

'I should say not,' said Gus. 'Sheer power, eh? Speed, ruthlessness, austerity, significant form, eh? Also' (and here he dropped his voice) 'very expensive indeed.'

Then he made John sit in the machine and he himself sat beside him. Then he began pulling the levers about and for a long time nothing happened: but at last there came a flash and a roar and the machine bounded into the air and then dashed forward. Before John had got his breath they had flashed across a broad thoroughfare which he recognized as the main road, and were racing through the country to the north of it—a flat country of square stony fields divided by barbed wire fences. A moment later they were standing still in a city where all the houses were built of steel.

BOOK THREE

THROUGH DARKEST ZEITGEISTHEIM

And every shrewd turn was exalted among men . . . and simple goodness, wherein nobility doth ever most participate, was mocked away and clean vanished.—

—THUCYDIDES

Now live the lesser, as lords of the world,
The busy troublers. Banished is our glory,
The earth's excellence grows old and sere.—ANON

The more ignorant men are, the more convinced are they that their little parish and their little chapel is an apex to which civilization and philosophy has painfully struggled up.—SHAW

CHAPTER ONE

Eschropolis

THEN I dreamed that he led John into a big room rather like a bathroom: it was full of steel and glass and the walls were nearly all window, and there was a crowd of people there, drinking what looked like medicine and talking at the tops of their voices. They were all either young, or dressed up to look as if they were young. The girls had short hair and flat breasts and flat buttocks so that they looked like boys: but the boys had pale, egg-shaped faces and slender waists and big hips so that they looked like girls—except for a few of them who had long hair and beards.

'What are they so angry about?' whispered John.

'They are not angry,' said Gus; 'they are talking about Art.'

Then he brought John into the middle of the room and said:

'Say! Here's a guy who has been taken in by my father and wants some real hundred per cent music to clean him out. We had better begin with something neo-romantic to make the transition.'

Then all the Clevers consulted together and presently they all agreed that Victoriana had better sing first. When Victoriana rose John at first thought that she was a schoolgirl: but after he had looked at her again he perceived that she was in fact about fifty. Before she began to sing she put on a dress which was a sort of exaggerated copy of Mr. Halfways' robes, and a mask which was like the Steward's mask except that the nose had been painted bright red and one of the eyes had been closed in a permanent wink.

'Priceless!' exclaimed one half of the Clevers, 'too Puritanian.'

But the other half, which included all the bearded men, held their noses in the air and looked very stiff. Then Victoriana took a little toy harp and began. The noises of the toy harp were so strange that John could not think of them as music at all. Then, when she sang, he had a picture in his mind which was a little like the Island, but he saw at once

that it was not the Island. And presently he saw people who looked
rather like his father, and the Steward and old Mr. Halfways, dressed
up as clowns and doing a stiff sort of dance. Then there was a colum-
bine, and some sort of love-story. But suddenly the whole Island
turned into an aspidistra in a pot and the song was over.

'Priceless,' said the Clevers.

'I hope you liked it,' said Gus to John.

'Well,' began John doubtfully, for he hardly knew what to say: but
he got no further, for at that moment he had a very great surprise.
Victoriana had thrown her mask away and walked up to him and
slapped him in the face twice, as hard as she could.

'That's right,' said the Clevers, 'Victoriana has *courage*. We may not
all agree with you, Vikky dear, but we admire your courage.'

'You may persecute me as much as you like,' said Victoriana to
John. 'No doubt to see me thus with my back to the wall, wakes the
hunting lust in you. You will always follow the cry of the majority.
But I will fight to the end. So there,' and she began to cry.

'I am extremely sorry,' said John. 'But——'

'And I *know* it was a good song,' sobbed Victoriana, 'because all
great singers are persecuted in their lifetime—and I'm per-persecuted—
and therefore I *must* be a great singer.'

'She has you there,' said the Clevers, as Victoriana left the laboratory.

'You mustn't mind her being a little bitter,' said Gus. 'She is so
temperamental and sensitive, and she has suffered a great deal.'

'Well, I must admit,' said one of the Clevers, 'now that she has
gone, that I think that stuff of hers rather *vieux jeu.*'

'Can't stand it myself,' said another.

'I think it was *her* face that needed slapping,' said a third.

'She's been spoiled and flattered all her life,' said a fourth. 'That's
what's the matter with her.'

'Quite,' said the rest in chorus.

CHAPTER TWO

A South Wind

'PERHAPS,' said Gus, 'someone else would give us a song.'

'I will,' cried thirty voices all together: but one cried much louder than the others and its owner had stepped into the middle of the room before anyone could do anything about it. He was one of the bearded men and wore nothing but a red shirt and a cod-piece made of the skins of crocodiles: and suddenly he began to beat on an African tom-tom and to croon with his voice, swaying his lean, half-clad body to and fro and staring at them all, out of eyes which were like burning coals. This time John saw no picture of an Island at all. He seemed to be in a dark green place full of tangled roots and hairy vegetable tubes: and all at once he saw in it shapes moving and writhing that were not vegetable but human. And the dark green grew darker, and a fierce heat came out of it: and suddenly all the shapes that were moving in the darkness came together to make a single obscene image which dominated the whole room. And the song was over.

'Priceless,' said the Clevers. 'Too stark! Too virile.' *Too much*

John blinked and looked round; and when he saw all the Clevers as cool as cucumbers, smoking their cigarettes and drinking the drinks that looked like medicines, all as if nothing remarkable had happened, he was troubled in his mind; for he thought that the song must have meant something different to them, and 'If so,' he argued, 'what very pure-minded people they must be.' Feeling himself among his betters, he became ashamed.

'You like it, *hein*?' said the bearded singer.

'I—I don't think I understood it,' said John.

'I make you like it, *hein*,' said the singer, snatching up his tom-tom again. 'It was what you *really* wanted all the time.'

'No, no,' cried John. 'I know you are wrong there. I grant you, that —that sort of thing—is what I always *get* if I think too long about the Island. But it can't be what I *want*.'

52

'No? Why not?'

'If it is what I wanted, why am I so disappointed when I get it? If what a man really wanted was food, how could he be disappointed when the food arrived? As well, I don't understand——'

'What you not understand? I explain to you.'

'Well, it's like this. I thought that you objected to Mr. Halfways' singing because it led to brown girls in the end.'

'So we do.'

'Well, why is it better to lead to black girls in the beginning?'

A low whistle ran round the whole laboratory. John knew he had made a horrible blunder.

'Look here,' said the bearded singer in a new voice, 'what do you mean? You are not suggesting that there is anything of that kind about my singing, are you?'

'I—I suppose—perhaps it was my fault,' stammered John.

'In other words,' said the singer, 'you are not yet able to distinguish between art and pornography!' and advancing towards John very deliberately, he spat in his face and turned to walk out of the room.

'That's right, Phally,' cried the Clevers, 'serve him right.'

'Filthy-minded little beast,' said one.

'Yah! Puritanian!' said a girl.

'I expect he's impotent,' whispered another.

'You mustn't be too hard on him,' said Gus. 'He is full of inhibi-tions and everything he says is only a rationalization of them. Perhaps he would get on better with something more formal. Why don't you sing, Glugly?'

CHAPTER THREE

Freedom of Thought

GLUGLY instantly rose. She was very tall and as lean as a post: and her mouth was not quite straight in her face. When she was in the middle of the room, and silence had been obtained, she began to make gestures. First of all she set her arms a-kimbo and cleverly turned her hands the wrong way so that it looked as if her wrists were sprained. Then she waddled to and fro with her toes pointing in. After that she twisted herself to make it look as if her hip bone was out of joint. Finally she made some grunts, and said:

'Globol obol oogle ogle globol gloogle gloo,' and ended by pursing up her lips and making a vulgar noise such as children make in their nurseries. Then she went back to her place and sat down.

'Thank you very much,' said John politely.

But Glugly made no reply, for Glugly could not talk, owing to an accident in infancy.

'I hoped you liked it,' said young Halfways.

'I didn't understand her.'

'Ah,' said a woman in spectacles who seemed to be Glugly's nurse or keeper, 'that is because you are looking for beauty. You are still thinking of your Island. You have got to realize that satire is the moving force in modern music.'

'It is the expression of a savage disillusionment,' said someone else.

'Reality has broken down,' said a fat boy who had drunk a great deal of the medicine and was lying flat on his back, smiling happily.

'Our art *must* be brutal,' said Glugly's nurse.

'We lost our ideals when there was a war in this country,' said a very young Clever, 'they were ground out of us in the mud and the flood and the blood. That is why we have to be so stark and brutal.'

'But, look here,' cried John, 'that war was years ago. It was your fathers who were in it: and they are all settled down and living ordinary lives.'

'Puritanian! Bourgeois!' cried the Clevers. Everyone seemed to have risen.

'Hold your tongue,' whispered Gus in John's ear. But already someone had struck John on the head, and as he bowed under the blow someone else hit him from behind.

'It was the mud and the blood,' hissed the girls all round him.

'Well,' said John, ducking to avoid a retort that had been flung at him, 'if you are really old enough to remember that war, why do you pretend to be so young?'

'We are young,' they howled; 'we are the new movement; we are the revolt.'

'We have got over humanitarianism,' bellowed one of the bearded men, kicking John on the kneecap.

'And prudery,' said a thin little old maid trying to wrench his clothes off from the neck. And at the same moment six girls leaped at his face with their nails, and he was kicked in the back and the belly, and tripped up so that he fell on his face, and hit again as he rose, and all the glass in the world seemed breaking round his head as he fled for his life from the laboratory. And all the dogs of Eschropolis joined in the chase as he ran along the street, and all the people followed pelting him with ordure, and crying:

'Puritanian! Bourgeois! Prurient!'

CHAPTER FOUR

The Man Behind the Gun

WHEN John could run no further he sat down. The noise of the pursuers had died away and, looking back, he could see no sign of Eschropolis. He was covered with filth and blood, and his breathing hurt him. There seemed to be something wrong with one of his wrists. As he was too tired to walk he sat still and thought for a while. And first he thought that he would like to go back to Mr. Halfways. 'It is true,' he said, 'that if you listened to him too long it would lead you to Media—and she *had* a trace of brown in her. But then you had a glimpse of the Island first. Now the Clevers took you straight to brown girls—or worse—without even a glimpse of the Island. I wonder would it be possible to keep always at the Island stage with Mr. Halfways? Must it always end like that?' Then it came into his head that after all he did not want Mr. Halfways' songs, but the Island itself: and that this was the only thing he wanted in the world. And when he remembered this he rose very painfully to continue his journey, looking round for the West. He was still in the flat country, but there seemed to be mountains ahead, and above them the sun was setting. A road ran towards them: so he began to limp along it. Soon the sunset disappeared and the sky was clouded over and a cold rain began.

When he had limped about a mile he passed a man who was mending the fence of his field and smoking a big cigar. John stopped and asked him if he knew the way to the sea.

'Nope,' said the man without looking up.

'Do you know of any place in this country where I could get a night's lodging?'

'Nope,' said the man.

'Could you give me a piece of bread?' said John.

'Certainly not,' said Mr. Mammon, 'it would be contrary to all economic laws. It would pauperize you.' Then, when John lingered, he added, 'Move on. I don't want any loiterers about here.'

John limped on for about ten minutes. Suddenly he heard Mr. Mammon calling out to him. He stopped and turned round.

'What do you want?' shouted John.

'Come back,' said Mr. Mammon.

John was so tired and hungry that he humbled himself to walk back (and the way seemed long) in the hope that Mammon had relented. When he came again to the place where they had talked before, the man finished his work without speaking and then said:

'Where did you get your clothes torn?'

'I had a quarrel with the Clevers in Eschropolis.'

'Clevers?'

'Don't you know them?'

'Never heard of them.'

'You know Eschropolis?'

'Know it? I *own* Eschropolis.'

'How do you mean?'

'What do you suppose they live on?'

'I never thought of that.'

'Every man of them earns his living by writing for me or having shares in my land. I suppose the "Clevers" is some nonsense they do in their spare time—when they're not beating up tramps,' and he glanced at John. Then he resumed his work.

'You needn't wait,' he said presently.

CHAPTER FIVE

Under Arrest

THEN I turned round and immediately began to dream again and I saw John plodding westward in the dark and the rain, in great distress, because he was too tired to go on and too cold to stop. And after a time there came a north wind that drove the rain away and skinned the puddles with ice and set the bare boughs clashing in the trees. And the moon came out. Now John looked up with his teeth chattering and saw that he was entering into a long valley of rocks with high cliffs on the right and the left. And the far end of the valley was barred with a high cliff all across except for one narrow pass in the middle. The moonlight lay white on this cliff and right amidst it was a huge shadow like a man's head. John glanced over his shoulder and saw that the shadow was thrown by a mountain behind him, which he had passed in the darkness.

It was far too cold for a man to stay still in the wind, and I dreamed of John going stumblingly forward up the valley till now he had come to the rock-wall and was about to enter the pass. But just as he rounded a great boulder and came full in sight of the pass he saw some armed men sitting in it by a brazier; and immediately they sprang up and barred his way.

'You can't pass here,' said their leader.

'Where can I pass?' said John.

'Where are you going to?'

'I am going to find the sea in order to set sail for an Island that I have seen in the West.'

'Then you cannot pass.'

'By whose orders?'

'Do you not know that all this country belongs to the Spirit of the Age?'

'I am sorry,' said John, 'I didn't know. I have no wish to trespass, I will go round some other way. I will not go through his country at all.'

'You fool,' said the captain, 'you are in his country *now*. This pass is the way out of it, not the way into it. He welcomes strangers. His quarrel is with runaways.' Then he called to one of his men and said, 'Here, Enlightenment, take this fugitive to our Master.'

A young man stepped out and clapped fetters upon John's hands: then putting the length of chain over his own shoulder and giving it a jerk he began to walk down the valley dragging John after him.

CHAPTER SIX

Poisoning the Wells

THEN I saw them going down the valley, the way John had come up, with the moon full in their faces: and up against the moon was the mountain which had cast the shadow, and now it looked more like a man than before.

'Mr. Enlightenment,' said John at last. 'Is it really you?'

'Why should it not be?' said the guard.

'You looked so different when I met you before.'

'We have never met before.'

'What? Did you not meet me at the inn on the borders of Puritania and drive me five miles in your pony trap?'

'Oh, *that*?' said the other. 'That must have been my father, old Mr. Enlightenment. He is a vain and ignorant old man, almost a Puritanian, and we never mention him in the family. I am Sigismund Enlightenment and I have long since quarrelled with my father.'

They went on in silence for a bit. Then Sigismund spoke again.

'It may save trouble if I tell you at once the best reason for not trying to escape: namely, that there is nowhere to escape to.'

'How do you know there is no such place as my Island?'

'Do you wish very much that there was?'

'I do.'

'Have you never before imagined anything to be true because you greatly wished for it?'

John thought for a little, and then he said 'Yes.'

'And your Island is *like* an imagination—isn't it?'

'I suppose so.'

'It is just the sort of thing you *would* imagine merely through wanting it—the whole thing is very suspicious. But answer me another question. Have you ever—ever once yet—had a vision of the Island that did not end in brown girls?'

'I don't know that I have. But they weren't what I wanted.'

'No. What you wanted was to have them, and with them, the satisfaction of feeling that you were good. Hence the Island.'

'You mean——'

'The Island was the pretence that you put up to conceal your own lusts from yourself.'

'All the same—I was disappointed when it ended like that.'

'Yes. You were disappointed at finding that you could not have it both ways. But you lost no time in having it the way you could: you did not reject the brown girls.'

They went on in silence for a time and always the mountain with its odd shape grew bigger in front of them; and now they were in its shadow. Then John spoke again, half in his sleep, for he was very tired.

'After all, it isn't only my Island. I might go back—back East and try the mountains.'

'The mountains do not exist.'

'How do you know?'

'Have you ever been there? Have you ever seen them except at night or in a blaze of sunrise?'

'No.'

'And your ancestors must have enjoyed thinking that when their leases were out they would go up to the mountains and live in the Landlord's castle—It is a more cheerful prospect than going—nowhere.'

'I suppose so.'

'It is clearly one more of the things people *wish* to believe.'

'But do we never do anything else? Are all the things I see at this moment there, only because I wish to see them.'

'Most of them,' said Sigismund. 'For example—you would like that thing in front of us to be a mountain; that is why you think it is a mountain.'

'Why?' cried John. 'What is it?'

And then in my nightmare I thought John became like a terrified child and put his hands over his eyes not to see the giant; but young Mr. Enlightenment tore his hands away and forced his face round and made him see the Spirit of the Age where it sat like one of the stone giants, the size of a mountain, with its eyes shut. Then Mr. Enlighten-ment opened a little door among the rocks and flung John into a pit made in the side of a hill, just opposite the giant, so that the giant could look into it through its gratings.

'He will open his eyes presently,' said Mr. Enlightenment. Then he locked the door and left John in prison.

CHAPTER SEVEN

Facing the Facts

JOHN lay in his fetters all night in the cold and stench of the dungeon. And when morning came there was a little light at the grating, and, looking round, John saw that he had many fellow prisoners, of all sexes and ages. But instead of speaking to him, they all huddled away from the light and drew as far back into the pit, away from the grating, as they could. But John thought that if he could breathe a little fresh air he would be better, and he crawled up to the grating. But as soon as he looked out and saw the giant, it crushed the heart out of him: and even as he looked, the giant began to open his eyes and John, without knowing why he did it, shrank from the grating. Now I dreamed that the giant's eyes had this property, that whatever they looked on became transparent. Consequently, when John looked round into the dun-geon, he retreated from his fellow prisoners in terror, for the place seemed to be thronged with demons. A woman was seated near him, but he did not know it was a woman, because, through the face, he saw the skull and through that the brains and the passages of the nose, and the larynx, and the saliva moving in the glands and the blood in the veins: and lower down the lungs panting like sponges, and the liver, and the intestines like a coil of snakes. And when he averted his eyes from her they fell on an old man, and this was worse for the old man had a cancer. And when John sat down and drooped his head, not to see the horrors, he saw only the working of his own inwards. Then I dreamed of all these creatures living in that hole under the giant's eye for many days and nights. And John looked round on it all and suddenly he fell on his face and thrust his hands into his eyes and cried out, 'It is the black hole. There may be no Landlord, but it is true about the black hole. I am mad. I am dead. I am in hell for ever.'

CHAPTER EIGHT

Parrot Disease

EVERY day a jailor brought the prisoners their food, and as he laid down the dishes he would say a word to them. If their meal was flesh he would remind them that they were eating corpses, or give them some account of the slaughtering: or, if it was the inwards of some beast, he would read them a lecture in anatomy and show the likeness of the mess to the same parts in themselves—which was the more easily done because the giant's eyes were always staring into the dungeon at dinner time. Or if the meal were eggs he would recall to them that they were eating the menstruum of a verminous fowl, and crack a few jokes with the female prisoners. So he went on day by day. Then I dreamed that one day there was nothing but milk for them, and the jailor said as he put down the pipkin:

'Our relations with the cow are not delicate—as you can easily see if you imagine eating any of her other secretions.'

Now John had been in the pit a shorter time than any of the others: and at these words something seemed to snap in his head and he gave a great sigh and suddenly spoke out in a loud, clear voice:

'Thank heaven! Now at last I know that you are talking nonsense.'

'What do you mean?' said the jailor, wheeling round upon him.

'You are trying to pretend that unlike things are like. You are trying to make us think that milk is the same sort of thing as sweat or dung.'

'And pray, what difference is there except by custom?'

'Are you a liar or only a fool, that you see no difference between that which Nature casts out as refuse and that which she stores up as food?'

'So Nature is a person, then, with purposes and consciousness,' said the jailor with a sneer. 'In fact, a Landlady. No doubt it comforts you to imagine you can believe that sort of thing;' and he turned to leave the prison with his nose in the air.

'I know nothing about that,' shouted John after him. 'I am talking of what happens. Milk does feed calves and dung does not.'

'Look here,' cried the jailor, coming back, 'we have had enough of this. It is high treason and I shall bring you before the Master.' Then he jerked John up by his chain and began to drag him towards the door; but John as he was being dragged, cried out to the others, 'Can't you see it's all a cheat?' Then the jailor struck him in the teeth so hard that his mouth was filled with blood and he became unable to speak: and while he was silent the jailor addressed the prisoners and said:

'You see he is trying to argue. Now tell me, someone, what is argument?'

There was a confused murmur.

'Come, come,' said the jailor. 'You must know your catechisms by now, You, there' (and he pointed to a prisoner little older than a boy whose name was Master Parrot), 'what is argument?'

'Argument,' said Master Parrot, 'is the attempted rationalization of the arguer's desires.'

'Very good,' replied the jailor, 'but you should turn out your toes and put your hands behind your back. That is better. Now: what is the proper answer to an argument proving the existence of the Landlord?'

'The proper answer is, "You say that because you are a Steward."'

'Good boy. But hold your head up. That's right. And what is the answer to an argument proving that Mr. Phally's songs are just as brown as Mr. Halfways'?'

'There are two only generally necessary to damnation,' said Master Parrot. 'The first is, "You say that because you are a Puritanian," and the second is, "You say that because you are a sensualist."'

'Good. Now just one more. What is the answer to an argument turning on the belief that two and two make four?'

'The answer is, "You say that because you are a mathematician," '

'You are a very good boy,' said the jailor. 'And when I come back I shall bring you something nice. And now for *you*,' he added, giving John a kick and opening the grating.

CHAPTER NINE

The Giant Slayer

WHEN they came out into the air John blinked a little, but not much, for they were still only in a half-light under the shadow of the giant, who was very angry, with smoke coming from his mouth, so that he looked more like a volcano than an ordinary mountain. And now John gave himself up for lost, but just as the jailor had dragged him up to the giant's feet, and had cleared his throat, and begun 'The case against this prisoner—' there was a commotion and a sound of horse's hoofs. The jailor looked round, and even the giant took his terrible eyes off John and looked round: and last of all, John himself looked round too. They saw some of the guard coming towards them leading a great black stallion, and in it was seated a figure wound in a cloak of blue which was hooded over the head and came down concealing the face.

'Another prisoner, Lord,' said the leader of the guards.

Then very slowly the giant raised his great, heavy finger and pointed to the mouth of the dungeon.

'Not yet,' said the hooded figure. Then suddenly it stretched out its hands with the fetters on them and made a quick movement of the wrists. There was a tinkling sound as the fragments of the broken chain fell on the rock at the horse's feet: and the guardsmen let go the bridle and fell back, watching. Then the rider threw back the cloak and a flash of steel smote light into John's eyes and on the giant's face. John saw that it was a woman in the flower of her age: she was so tall that she seemed to him a Titaness, a sun-bright virgin clad in complete

63

steel, with a sword naked in her hand. The giant bent forward in his chair and looked at her.

'Who are you?' he said.

'My name is Reason,' said the virgin.

'Make out her passport quickly,' said the giant in a low voice. 'And let her go through our dominions and be off with all the speed she wishes.'

'Not yet,' said Reason. 'I will ask you three riddles before I go, for a wager.'

'What is the pledge?' said the giant.

'Your head,' said Reason.

There was silence for a time among the mountains.

'Well,' said the giant at last, 'what must be, must be. Ask on.'

'This is my first riddle,' said Reason. 'What is the colour of things in dark places, of fish in the depth of the sea, or of the entrails in the body of man?'

'I cannot say,' said the giant.

'Well,' said Reason. 'Now hear my second riddle. There was a certain man who was going to his own house and his enemy went with him. And his house was beyond a river too swift to swim and too deep to wade. And he could go no faster than his enemy. While he was on his journey his wife sent to him and said, You know that there is only one bridge across the river: tell me, shall I destroy it that the enemy may not cross; or shall I leave it standing that you may cross? What should this man do?'

'It is too hard for me,' said the giant.

'Well,' said Reason. 'Try now to answer my third riddle. By what rule do you tell a copy from an original?'

The giant muttered and mumbled and could not answer, and Reason set spurs in her stallion and it leaped up on to the giant's mossy knees and galloped up his foreleg, till she plunged her sword into his heart. Then there was a noise and a crumbling like a landslide and the huge carcass settled down: and the Spirit of the Age became what he had seemed to be at first, a sprawling hummock of rock.

BOOK FOUR

BACK TO THE ROAD

Doth any man doubt, that if there were taken out of men's minds vain opinions, flattering hopes, false valuations, imaginations as one would, and the like: but it would leave the minds of a number of men poor shrunken things: full of melancholy and indisposition, and unpleasing to themselves?—BACON

But those who have been Freudianised too long are incurable

CHAPTER ONE

Let Grill be Grill

THE guards had fled. Reason dismounted from her horse and wiped her sword clean on the moss of the foot hills which had been the giant's knees. Then she turned to the door of the pit and struck it so that it broke and she could look into the darkness of the pit and smell the filth.

'You can all come out,' she said.

But there was no movement from within: only, John could hear the prisoners wailing together and saying:

'It is one more wish-fulfilment dream: it is one more wish-fulfilment dream. Don't be taken in again.'

But presently Master Parrot came to the mouth of the pit and said, 'There is no good trying to fool us. Once bit twice shy.' Then he put out his tongue and retired.

'This psittacosis is a very obstinate disorder,' said Reason. And she turned to mount the black horse.

'May I come with you, lady?' said John.

'You may come until you are tired,' said Reason.

CHAPTER TWO

Archtype and Ectype

IN my dream I saw them set off together, John walking by the lady's stirrup: and I saw them go up the rocky valley where John had gone on the night of his capture. They found the pass unguarded and it gave back an echo to the horse's hoofs and then in a moment they were out of the mountain country and going down a grassy slope into the land beyond. There were few trees and bare, and it was cold: but presently John looked aside and saw a crocus in the grass. For the first time for many days the old sweetness pierced through John's heart: and the next moment he was trying to call back the sound of the birds wheeling over the Island and the green of the waves breaking on its sand—for they had all flashed about him but so quickly that they were gone before he knew. His eyes were wet.

He turned to Reason and spoke.

'You can tell me, lady. Is there such a place as the Island in the West, or is it only a feeling of my own mind?'

'I cannot tell you,' said she, 'because you do not know.'

'But you know.'

'But I can tell you only what *you* know. I can bring things out of the dark part of your mind into the light part of it. But now you ask me what is not even in the dark part of your mind.'

'Even if it were only a feeling in my own mind, would it be a bad feeling?'

'I have nothing to tell you of good and bad.'

'I mean this,' said John. 'And this you can tell me. Is it true that it must always end in brown girls, or rather, that it really *begins* from brown girls? They say it is all a pretence, all a disguise for lust.'

'And what do you think of that saying?'

'It is very like that,' said John. 'Both are sweet. Both are full of longing. The one runs into the other. They *are* very alike.'

'Indeed they are,' said the lady. 'But do you not remember my third riddle?'

'About the copy and the original? I could not understand it.'

'Well, now you shall. The people in the country we have just left have seen that your love for the Island is very like your love for the brown girls. Therefore they say that one is a copy of the other. They would also say that you have followed me because I am like your mother, and that your trust in me is a copy of your love for your mother. And then they would say again that your love for your mother is a copy of your love for the brown girls; and so they would come full circle.'

'And what should I answer them?'

'You would say, perhaps one is a copy of the other. But which is the copy of which?'

'I never thought of that.'

'You are not yet of an age to have thought much,' said Reason. 'But you must see that if two things are alike, then it is a further question whether the first is copied from the second, or the second from the first, or both from a third.'

'What would the third be?'

'Some have thought that all these loves were copies of our love for the Landlord.'

'But surely they have considered that and rejected it. Their sciences have disproved it.'

'They could not have, for their sciences are not concerned at all with the general relations of this country to anything that may lie East of it or West of it. They indeed will tell you that their researches have proved that if two things are similar, the fair one is always the copy of the foul one. But their only reason to say so is that they have already decided that the fairest things of all—that is the Landlord, and, if you like, the mountains and the Island—are a mere copy of *this* country. They pretend that their researches lead to that doctrine: but in fact they assume that doctrine first and interpret their researches by it.'

'But they have reasons for assuming it.'

'They have none, for they have ceased to listen to the only people who can tell them anything about it.'

'Who are they?'

'They are younger sisters of mine, and their names are Philosophy and Theology.'

'Sisters! Who is your father?'

'You will know sooner than you wish.'

And now the evening was falling and they were near a little farm, so they turned in there and asked a night's lodging of the farmer, which was readily given them.

CHAPTER THREE

Esse is Percipi

NEXT morning they continued their journey together. In my dream I saw them go through a country of little hills where the road was always

68

winding to conform to the lie of the valleys: and John walked at the lady's stirrup. The fetter of his hands had broken at the moment when she killed the giant, but the handcuffs were still on his wrists. One half of the broken chain hung down from each hand. There was a greater mildness in the air this day and the buds were fully formed in the hedges.

'I have been thinking, lady,' said John, 'of what you said yesterday and I think I understand that though the Island is very like the place where I first met the brown girl, yet she might be the shadow and the Island the reality. But there is one thing that troubles me.'

'What is that?' said Reason.

'I cannot forget what I have seen in the giant's prison. If we are really like that inside, whatever we imagine must be abominable however innocent it looks. It may be true in general that the foul thing is not always the original and the fair thing not always the copy. But when we have to do with human imaginations, with things that come out of *us*, surely then the giant is right? There at least it is much more likely that whatever seems good is only a veil for the bad—only a part of our skin that has so far escaped the giant's eyes and not yet become trans, parent.'

'There are two things to be said about that,' replied the lady, 'and the first is this. Who told you that the Island was an imagination of yours?'

'Well, you would not assure me that it was anything real.'

'Nor that it was not.'

'But I must think it is one or the other.'

'By my father's soul, you must *not*—until you have some evidence. Can you not remain in doubt?'

'I don't know that I have ever tried.'

'You must learn to, if you are to come far with me. It is not hard to do it. In Eschropolis, indeed, it is impossible, for the people who live there have to give an opinion once a week or once a day, or else Mr. Mammon would soon cut off their food. But out here in the country you can walk all day and all the next day with an unanswered question in your head: you need never speak until you have made up your mind.'

'But if a man wanted to know so badly that he would die unless the question was decided—and no more evidence turned up.'

'Then he would die, that would be all.'

They went on in silence for à while.

'You said there were two things to say,' said John. 'What was the second?'

'The second was this. Did you think that the things you saw in the dungeon were *real*: that we really are like that?'

'Of course I did. It is only our skin that hides them.'

'Then I must ask you the same question that I asked the giant. 'What is the colour of things in the dark?'

'I suppose, no colour at all.'

'And what of their shape? Have you any notion of it save as what could be seen or touched, or what you could collect from many seeings and touchings?'

'I don't know that I have.'

'Then do you not see how the giant has deceived you?'

'Not quite clearly.'

'He showed you by a trick what our inwards *would* look like if they were visible. That is, he showed you something that is not, but some- thing that would be if the world were made all other than it is. But in the real world our inwards are invisible. They are not coloured shapes at all, they are feelings. The warmth in your limbs at this moment, the sweetness of your breath as you draw it in, the comfort in your belly because we breakfasted well, and your hunger for the next meal— these are the reality: all the sponges and tubes that you saw in the dungeon are the lie.'

'But if I cut a man open I should see them in him.'

'A man cut open is, so far, not a man: and if you did not sew him up speedily you would be seeing not organs, but death. I am not denying that death is ugly: but the giant made you believe that life is ugly.'

'I cannot forget the man with the cancer.'

'What you saw was unreality. The ugly lump was the giant's trick: the reality was pain, which has no colour or shape.'

'Is that much better?'

'That depends on the man.'

'I think I begin to see.'

'Is it surprising that things should look strange if you see them as they are not? If you take an organ out of a man's body—or a longing out of the dark part of a man's mind—and give to the one the shape and colour, and to the other the self-consciousness, which they never have in reality, would you expect them to be other than monstrous?'

'Is there, then, no truth at all in what I saw under the giant's eyes?'

'Such pictures are useful to physicians.'

'Then I really am clean,' said John. 'I am not—like those.'

Reason smiled. 'There, too,' she said, 'there is truth mixed up with the giant's conjuring tricks. It will do you no harm to remember from time to time the ugly sights inside. You come of a race that cannot afford to be proud.'

As she spoke John looked up, in doubt of her meaning: and for the first time since he came into her company he felt afraid. But the impression lasted only for a moment. 'Look,' said John, 'here is a little inn. Is it not time that we rested and ate something?'

CHAPTER FOUR

Escape

In the warmth of the afternoon they went on again, and it came into John's mind to ask the lady the meaning of her second riddle.

'It has two meanings,' said she, 'and in the first the bridge signifies Reasoning. The Spirit of the Age wishes to allow argument and not to allow argument.'

'How is that?'

'You heard what they said. If anyone argues with them they say that he is rationalizing his own desires, and therefore need not be answered. But if anyone listens to them they will then argue themselves to show that their own doctrines are true.'

'I see. And what is the cure for this?'

'You must ask them whether any reasoning is valid or not. If they say no, then their own doctrines, being reached by reasoning, fall to the ground. If they say yes, then they will have to examine your arguments and refute them on their merits: for if some reasoning is valid, for all they know, your bit of reasoning may be one of the valid bits.'

'I see,' said John. 'But what was the second interpretation?'

'In the second,' said Reason, 'the bridge signifies the giant's own favourite doctrine of the wish-fulfilment dream. For this also he wishes to use and not to use.'

'I don't see how he wishes *not* to use it.'

'Does he not keep on telling people that the Landlord is a wish-fulfilment dream?'

'Yes; surely that is true—the only true thing he did say.'

'Now think. Is it really true that the giant and Sigismund, and the people in Eschropolis, and Mr. Halfways, are going about filled with a longing that there should be a Landlord, and cards of rules, and a mountain land beyond the brook, with a possibility of a black hole?'

Then John stood still on the road to think. And first he gave a shake of his shoulders, and then he put his hands to his sides, and then he began to laugh till he was almost shaken to pieces. And when he had nearly finished, the vastness and impudence and simplicity of the fraud which had been practised came over him all again, and he laughed harder. And just when he had nearly recovered and was beginning to get his breath again, suddenly he had a picture in his mind of Victoriana and Glugly and Gus Halfways and how they would look if a rumour reached them that there *was* a Landlord and he was coming to Eschropolis. This was too much for him, and he laughed so hard that the broken chains of the Spirit of the Age fell off his wrists altogether. But all the while Reason sat and watched him.

'You had better hear the rest of the argument,' she said at last. 'It may not be such a laughing matter as you suppose.'

'Oh, yes—the argument,' said John, wiping his eyes.

'You see now the direction in which the giant does *not* want the wish-fulfilment theory used?'

'I'm not sure that I do,' said John.

'Don't you see what follows if you adopt his own rules?'

'No,' said John, very loudly: for a terrible apprehension was stealing over him.

'But you must see,' said Reason, 'that for him and all his subjects *disbelief* in the Landlord is a wish-fulfilment dream.'

'I shall not adopt his rules.'

'You would be foolish not to have profited *at all* by your stay in his country,' said Reason. 'There is some force in the wish-fulfilment doctrine.'

'Some, perhaps, but very little.'

'I only wanted to make it clear that whatever force it had was in favour of the Landlord's existence, not against it—specially in your case.'

'Why specially in mine?' said John sulkily.

'Because the Landlord is the thing you have been most afraid of all your life. I do not say that any theory should be accepted because it is disagreeable, but if any should, then belief in the Landlord should be accepted first.'

As Reason said these words they had reached the top of a little hill, and John begged for a halt, being out of breath. He looked back and saw beyond the green, rolling country the dark line of mountains which was the frontier of the giant's land: but behind them, and far bigger, rose the old mountains of the East, picked out in the rays of the declining sun against a dark sky. They seemed no smaller than when John had looked at them long ago from Puritania.

'I do not know where you are leading me,' he said at last, 'and among all these winding roads I have lost my sense of direction. As well, I find the pace of your horse fatiguing. If you will excuse me, I think I will henceforth pursue my journey alone.'

'As you wish,' said Reason. 'But I would strongly advise you to take this turn to the left.'

'Where does it go to?' asked John suspiciously.

'It takes you back to the main road,' said Reason.

'That will do well enough,' said John, 'And now, lady, give me your blessing before I go.'

'I have no blessing to give,' said the Virgin. 'I do not deal in blessings and cursings.'

73

Then John bade her good-bye and took the road she had pointed out to him. As soon as she was out of sight, I dreamed that he put down his head and ran; for the silly fellow supposed that she might follow him. And he continued running until he found that he was going up a hill—a hill so steep that it left him no breath for running—and at the very top his road cut into another which ran left and right along the ridge. Then John looked one way along it to the East and the other way along it to the West, and saw that it was indeed the main road. He stayed for a minute to mop his brow. Then he turned to the right, with his face towards the setting sun, and resumed his journey.

BOOK FIVE

THE GRAND CANYON

Not by road and foot nor by sail and ocean
Shalt thou find any course that reaches
The world beyond the North.—PINDAR

The ephemerals have no help to give. Behold them;
They are deedless and cripple, like to
A dream. The kind of mortals
Is bound with a chain and their eyes are in darkness.—AESCHYLUS

Alas, what can they teach and not mislead,
Ignorant of themselves, of God much more,
And how the world began, and how man fell.—MILTON

CHAPTER ONE

The Grand Canyon

THE main road soon began to ascend and after a short climb John found himself on a bleak tableland which continued to rise before him, but at a gentler angle. After he had walked a mile or so he saw the figure of a man ahead, outlined against the setting sun. At first the figure stood still: then it took a few paces to the left and to the right as if in indecision. Then it turned about to face him, and to his surprise hailed him as an old acquaintance. Because of the light in his face John could not at first see who it was, and they had joined hands before he knew that it was Vertue.

'What can have delayed you?' cried John, 'I thought by your pace when I left you that you would have been a week's journey ahead of me by now.'

'If you think that,' said Vertue, 'your way must have been easier than mine. Have you not crossed mountains?'

'I came through a pass,' said John.

'The main road took them without a bend,' said Vertue. 'And I often made scarcely ten miles a day. But that does not signify: I have learned something of climbing and sweated off a good deal of soft flesh. What has really delayed me is this—I have been here for several days.'

With that he motioned John to proceed and they went forward together to the brow of the slope. Then I saw John start back a pace or so with a cry, for he had found that he stood on the edge of a precipice. Then presently he re-approached it with caution and looked.

He saw that the road ran up without warning to the edge of a great gorge or chasm and ended in the air, as if it had been broken off. The chasm might be seven miles wide and as for its length, it stretched southward on his left and northward on his right as far as he could see. The sun shining in his face cast all the further side into shadow, so that he could not see much of it clearly. It seemed to him, however, a rich country from the verdure and the size of the trees.

'I have been exploring the cliffs,' said Vertue. 'And I think we could get half-way down. Come a little nearer. You see that ledge?'

'I have a very poor head for heights,' said John.

'That one,' said Vertue, pointing to a narrow strip of greenery a thousand feet below them.

'I could never reach it.'

'Oh, you could reach *that* easily enough. The difficulty is to know what happens beyond it. I am inclined to think that it overhangs: and though we could get down to it, I am not sure that we could get back if the rest of the descent was impracticable.'

'Then it would be madness to trust ourselves so far.'

'I don't know about that. It would be in accordance with the rule.'

'What rule?'

'The rule is,' said Vertue, 'that if we have one chance out of a hundred of surviving, we must attempt it: but if we have none, absolutely none, then it would be self-destruction, and we need not.'

'It is no rule of mine,' said John.

'But it is. We all have the same set of rules, really, you know.'

'If it is a rule of mine, it is one that I cannot obey.'

'I don't think I understand you,' said Vertue. 'But of course you may be such a bad climber that *you* wouldn't have even one chance . . . that would make a difference, I allow.'

Then a third voice spoke.

'You have neither of you any chance at all unless I carry you down.'

Both the young men turned at the sound. An old woman was seated in a kind of rocky chair at the very edge of the precipice.

'Oh, it's you, Mother Kirk, is it?' said Vertue, and added in an undertone to John, 'I have seen her about the cliffs more than once. Some of the country people say she is second-sighted, and some that she is crazy.'

'I shouldn't trust her,' said John in the same tone. 'She looks to me much more like a witch.' Then he turned to the old woman and said aloud: 'And how could you carry us down, mother? We would be more fit to carry you.'

'I could do it, though,' said Mother Kirk, 'by the power that the Landlord has given me.'

'So you believe in the Landlord, too?' said John.

'How can I not, dear,' said she, 'when I am his own daughter-in-law?'

'He does not give you very fine clothes,' said John, glancing at the old woman's country cloak.

'They'll last my time,' said the old woman placidly.

'We ought to try her,' whispered Vertue to John. 'As long as there is any chance we are not allowed to neglect it.' But John frowned at him to be silent and addressed the old woman again.

'Do you not think this Landlord of yours is a very strange one?' he said.

'How so?' said she.

'Why does he make a road like this running up to the very edge of a precipice—unless it is to encourage travellers to break their necks in the dark?'

'Oh, bless you, he never left it like that,' said the old woman. 'It was a good road all round the world when it was new, and all this gorge is far later than the road.'

'You mean,' said Vertue, 'that there has been some sort of catastrophe.'

'Well,' said Mother Kirk, 'I see there will be no getting you down to-night, so I may as well tell you the story. Come and sit down by me. You are neither of you so wise that you need be ashamed of listening to an old wives' tale.'

CHAPTER TWO

Mother Kirk's Story

WHEN they were seated, the old woman told the following story:—

'You must know that once upon a time there were no tenants in this country at all, for the Landlord used to farm it himself. There were only the animals and the Landlord used to look after them, he and his sons and daughters. Every morning they used to come down from the mountains and milk the cows and lead out the sheep to pasture. And they needed less watching, for all the animals were tamer then; and there were no fences needed, for if a wolf got in among the flocks he would do them no harm. And one day the Landlord was going home from his day's work when he looked round on the country, and the beasts, and saw how the crops were springing, and it came into his head that the whole thing was too good to keep to himself. So he decided to let the country to tenants, and his first tenant was a young married man. But first the Landlord made a farm in the very centre of the land where the soil was the best and the air most wholesome, and that was the very spot where you are sitting now. They were to have the whole land, but that was too much for them to keep under cultivation. The Landlord's idea was that they could work the farm and leave the rest as a park for the time being: but later they could divide the park up into holdings for their children. For you must know that he drew up a very different lease from the kind you have nowadays. It was a lease in perpetuity on his side, for he promised never to turn them out; but on their side, they could leave when they chose, as long as one of their sons was there, to take the farm on, and then they could go up to live with him in the mountains. He thought that would be a good thing because it would broaden the minds of his own mountain children to mix with strangers. And they thought so too. But before he put the tenants in possession there was one thing he had to do. Up to this time the country had been full of a certain fruit which the Landlord had planted for the refreshment of himself and his children, if they were thirsty during the day as they worked down here. It was a very good fruit and up in the mountains they say it is even more plentiful: but it is very strong and only those who are mountain-bred ought to eat it, for only they can digest it properly. Hitherto, while there were only beasts in the land, it had done no harm for these mountain-apples to be growing in every thicket; for you know that an animal will eat nothing but what it is good for it. But now that there were to be men in the land, the Landlord was afraid that they might do themselves an injury; yet it was not to be thought of that he should dig up every sapling of that tree and make the country into a desert. So he decided that it was best to be frank with the young people, and when he found a great big mountain-apple tree growing in the very centre of the farm he said, "So much the better. If they are to learn sense, they may as well

79

learn it from the beginning: and if they will not, there's no help for it.
For if they did not find mountain apples on the farm, they would soon
find them somewhere else." So he left the apple tree standing, and put
the man and his wife into their farm: but before he left them he explained the whole affair to them—as much of it could be explained—
and warned them on no account to eat any of the apples. Then he went
home. And for a time the young man and his wife behaved very well,
tending the animals and managing their farm, and abstaining from the
mountain apples; and for all I know they might never have done
otherwise if the wife had not somehow made a new acquiantance. This
new acquaintance was a landowner himself. He had been born in the
mountains and was one of our Landlord's own children, but he had
quarrelled with his father and set up on his own, and now had built up
a very considerable estate in another country, His estate marches,
however, with this country: and as he was a great land-grabber he
always wanted to take this bit in—and he has very nearly succeeded.'

'I've never met any tenants of his,' said John.

'Not tenants in chief, my dear,' said the old woman. 'And so you
didn't know them. But you may have met the Clevers, who are tenants
of Mr. Mammon: and he is a tenant of the Spirit of the Age: who holds
directly of the Enemy.'

'I am sure the Clevers would be very surprised,' said John, 'to hear
that they had a Landlord at all. They would think this enemy, as you
call him, no less a superstition than *your* Landlord.'

'But that is how business is managed,' said Mother Kirk. 'The little
people do not know the big people to whom they belong. The big
people do not intend that they should. No important transference of
property could be carried out if all the small people at the bottom knew
what was really happening. But this is not part of my story. As I was
saying, the enemy got to know the farmer's wife: and, however he did
it, or whatever he said to her, it wasn't long before he persuaded her
that the one thing she needed was a nice mountain apple. And she
took one and ate it. And then—you know how it is with husbands—
she made the farmer come round to her mind. And at the moment he
put out his hand and plucked the fruit there was an earthquake, and
the country cracked open all the way across from North to South: and

80

ever since, instead of the farm, there has been this gorge, which the country people call the Grand Canyon. But in my language its name is *Peccatum Adae.*'

CHAPTER THREE

The Self-Sufficiency of Vertue

'AND I suppose,' said John sourly, 'the Landlord was so annoyed that it was he who invented the rules and the black hole?'

'The story is not quite so simple as that,' said the old woman, 'so many things happened after the eating of the apple. For one thing, the taste created such a craving in the man and the woman that they thought they could never eat enough of it; and they were not content with all the wild apple trees, but planted more and more, and grafted mountain-apple on to every other kind of tree so that every fruit should have a dash of that taste in it. They succeeded so well that the whole vegetable system of the country is now infected: and there is hardly a fruit or a root in the land—certainly none this side of the canyon—that has not a little mountain-apple in it. You have never tasted anything that was quite free from it.'

'And what has that got to do with the card of rules?' said John.

'Everything,' said Mother Kirk. 'In a country where all the food is more or less poisoned—but some of it very much less than more—you need very complicated rules indeed to keep healthy.'

'Meanwhile,' said Vertue, 'we are not getting on with our journey.'

'I will carry you down in the morning, if you like,' said Mother Kirk. 'Only mind you, it is a dangerous place, and you must do exactly as I tell you.'

'If the place is so dangerous——' began John, when Vertue, who had been struck by the woman's last words, suddenly broke in:

'I am afraid it is no use, mother,' he said; 'I cannot put myself under anyone's orders. I must be the captain of my soul and the master of my fate. But thank you for your offer.'

'You are right,' said John hastily, and added in a whisper, 'The old creature is clearly insane. Our real business is to explore this chasm North and South until we find some place where the descent *is* practicable.'

Vertue had risen.

'We are thinking, mother,' he said, 'that we should like to make sure for ourselves that there is no place where we cannot get down without being carried. You see my own legs have served me so far—and I should not like to start being carried now.'

'It will do you no harm to try,' answered Mother Kirk. 'And I should not wonder if you find a way down. Getting up the other side is another question, to be sure; but perhaps we shall meet again when it comes to that.'

By this time it was quite dark. The two young men bade good night to the woman and drew back along the main road to discuss their plans. Two by-roads branched off from it about a quarter of a mile from the precipice: and as that which went to the north seemed rather the better, and also pointed a little backward and away from the cliffs (which John was anxious not to skirt in the darkness), they turned northward. It was a fine starlit night and grew colder as they proceeded.

CHAPTER FOUR

Mr. Sensible

WHEN they had walked rather more than a mile John drew Vertue's attention to a light a little back from the road: and I saw them follow it till they came to a gateway and after that to a door, and there they knocked.

'Whose house is this?' said Vertue when the servant opened to them.

'This is Mr. Sensible's house,' said the servant. 'And if you are benighted travellers he will receive you gladly.'

Then he brought them into a room where a lamp was burning clearly, but not very brightly, and an old gentleman was seated by a blazing wood fire with his dog at his feet and his book on his knees and a jig-saw puzzle at one side of him spread out on a wooden frame, and on the other a chessboard with the pieces set for a problem. He rose to greet them very cordially but not hastily.

'You are very welcome, gentlemen,' said Mr. Sensible. 'Pray come and warm yourselves. Drudge' (and here he called to the servant) 'make some supper ready for three: the usual supper, Drudge. I shall not be able to offer you luxury, gentlemen. The wine of my own country, cowslip wine, shall be your drink. It will be rough to your palates, but to mine the draught that I owe to my own garden and my own kitchen will always have a flavour beyond Hippocrene. The radishes, also of my own growing, I think I may venture to praise. But I see by your looks that I have already betrayed my foible. I confess that my garden is my pride. But what then? We are all children, and I reckon him the wisest among us that can make most sport out of the toys suitable to that condition, without seeking to go beyond it. *Regum æquabit opes animis.* Contentment, my friends, contentment is the best riches. Do not let the dog tease you, sir. He has mange. Down, Rover! Alas, Rover! thou little knowest that sentence is passed upon thee.'

'You are surely not going to destroy him, sir?' said John.

'He begins to ail,' said Mr. Sensible. 'And it would be foolish to keep him longer. What would you? *Omnes eodem cogimur.* He has lain in the sun and hunted fleas enough, and now, poor fellow, he must go *quo dives Tullus et Ancus.* We must take life on the terms it is given us.'

'You will miss your old companion.'

'Why, as to that you know, the great art of life is to moderate our passions. Objects of affection are like other belongings. We must love them enough to enrich our lives while we have them—not enough to impoverish our lives when they are gone. You see this puzzle here. While I am engaged on it it seems to me of sovereign importance to fit the pieces together: when it is done I think of it no more: and if I should fail to do it, why I would not break my heart. Confound that Drudge. Hi! whoreson, are we to wait all night for our supper?'

'Coming, sir,' said Drudge from the kitchen.

'I think the fellow goes to sleep over his pots and pans,' said Mr. Sensible, 'but let us occupy the time by continuing our conversation. Good conversation I reckon among the finer sweets of life. But I would not include diatribe or lecturing or persistent discussion under that head. Your doctrinaire is the bane of all talk. As I sit here listening to your opinions—*nullius addictus*—and following the ball wherever it rolls, I defy system. I love to explore your minds *en deshabille*. Nothing comes amiss—*j'aime le jeu, l'amour, les livres, la musique, la ville et la champagne—enfin tout!* Chance is, after all, our best guide—need I call a better witness than the fortunate cast of the dice which has brought you beneath my roof to-night?'

'It wasn't exactly chance,' said Vertue, who had been restlessly waiting to speak. 'We are on a journey and we are looking for a way to cross the Grand Canyon.'

'*Haud equidem invideo,*' said the old gentleman. 'You do not insist on my accompanying you?'

'We hadn't thought of it,' said John.

'Why then I am very willing that you should go!' cried Mr. Sensible with a burst of melodious laughter. 'And yet to what end? I often amuse myself with speculating on that curious restlessness in the mind which drives us, specially in youth, to climb up a mountain merely in order that we may then climb down, or to cross the seas in order that we may pay an inn-keeper for setting before us worse cheer than we might eat in our own house. *Caelum non animum mutamus.* Not that I would repress the impulse, you understand, any more than I would starve any other part of my nature. Here again, the secret of happiness lies in knowing where to stop. A moderate allowance of travelling—enough to quiet, without satiating, a liberal curiosity—is very well. One brings back a few rarities to store in one's inner cabinet against a dull day. But the Grand Canyon—surely a modest tour along the cliffs on *this* side of it would give you much the same sort of scenery, and save your necks.'

'It wasn't scenery we were looking for,' said John. 'I am trying to find the Island in the West.'

'You refer, no doubt, to some æsthetic experience. There again—I would not urge a young man to shut his eyes to that sort of thing. Who has not felt immortal longings at the lengthening of the shadow or the turning of the leaf? Who has not stretched out his hands for the ulterior shore? *Et ego in Arcadia!* We have all been fools once—aye, and are

84

glad to have been fools too. But our imaginations, like our appetites, need discipline: not, heaven help us, in the interest of any transcenden‑ tal ethic, but in the interests of our own solid good. That wild impulse must be tasted, not obeyed. The bees have stings, but we rob them of their honey. To hold all that urgent sweetness to our lips in the cup of one perfect moment, missing no faintest ingredient in the flavour of its μονόχρονος ἡδονή, yet ourselves, in a sense, unmoved—this is the true art. This tames in the service of the reasonable life even those pleasures whose loss might seem to be the heaviest, yet necessary, price we paid for rationality. Is it an audacity to hint that for the corrected palate the taste of the draught even owes its last sweetness to the knowledge that we have wrested it from an unwilling source? To cut off pleasures from the consequences and conditions which they have by nature, detaching, as it were, the precious phrase from its irrelevant context, is what distinguishes the man from the brute and the citizen from the savage. I cannot join with those moralists who inveigh against the Roman emetics in their banquets: still less with those who would forbid the even more beneficent contraceptive devices of our later times. That man who can eat as taste, not nature, prompts him and yet fear no aching belly, or who can indulge in Venus and fear no imperti‑ nent bastard, is a civilized man. In him I recognize Urbanity—the note of the centre.'

'Do you know of any way across the canyon?' said Vertue abruptly.

'I do not,' said their host, 'for I have never made inquiries. The proper study of mankind is man, and I have always left useless specu‑ lations alone. Suppose that there were a way across, to what purpose should I use it? Why should I scramble down this side and up the other to find after my labours the same soil still beneath me and the same heaven above? It would be laughable to suppose that the country beyond the gorge can be any different from the country on this side of it. *Eadem sunt omnia semper.* Nature had already done all she can for our comfort and amusement, and the man who does not find content at home will seek it vainly abroad. Confound that fellow! Drudge! ! Will you bring us our supper or do you prefer to have every bone in your body broken?'

'Coming, sir,' said Drudge from the kitchen.

'There might be different *people* on the other side of the canyon,' suggested John in the momentary pause that followed.

'That is even less likely,' said Mr. Sensible. 'Human nature is always the same. The dress and the manners may vary, but I detect the unchanging heart beneath the shifting disguises. If there are men beyond the canyon, rest assured that we know them already. They are born and they die: and in the interval between they are the same lovable rascals that we know at home.'

'Still,' said John, 'you can't really be certain that there is no such place as my Island. Reason left it an open question.'

'Reason!' exclaimed Mr. Sensible. 'Do you mean the mad woman who goes riding about the country dressed up in armour? I trust that when I spoke of the reasonable life you did not think that I meant anything under *her* auspices? There is a strange confusion in our language here, for the reasonableness which I commend has no more dangerous enemy than Reason. Perhaps I should drop the use of the name altogether, and say that my deity is not reason but *le bon sens*.'

'What is the difference?' said Vertue.

'Sense is easy, Reason is hard. Sense knows where to stop with gracious inconsistency, while Reason slavishly follows an abstract logic whither she knows not. The one seeks comfort and finds it, the other seeks truth and is still seeking. *Le bon sens* is the father of a flourishing family: Reason is barren and a virgin. If I had my way I should clap this Reason of yours in the bridewell to pursue her meditations in the straw. The baggage has a pretty face, I allow: but she leads us from our true aim—joy, pleasure, ease, content, whate'er the name! She is a fanatic who has never learned from my master to pursue the golden mean, and, being a mortal, to think mortal thoughts. *Auream quisquis*——'

'It is very odd that you should say that,' interrupted Vertue, 'for I also was brought up on Aristotle. But I think my text must have differed from yours. In mine, the doctrine of the Mean does not bear the sense you have given it at all. He specially says that there is no excess of goodness. You cannot go too far in the right direction. The line that we should follow may start from a middle point in the base of a triangle: but the further off the apex is, the better. In that dimension——'

'*Do manus!*' broke out Mr. Sensible. 'Spare us the rest, young man. We are not at a lecture, and I readily admit that your scholarship is more recent than mine. Philosophy should be our mistress, not our master: and the pursuit of a pedantic accuracy amidst the freedom of our social pleasures is as unwelcome as——'

'And the bit about thinking mortal thoughts,' continued Vertue, whose social experience, as I dreamed, was not extensive, 'the bit about mortal thoughts was quoted by Aristotle to say that he disagreed with it. He held that the end of mortal life was to put on immortality as much as might be. And he also said that the most useless of studies was the noblest.'

'I see you are letter-perfect, young man,' said Mr. Sensible, with a rather chilly smile, 'and I am sure these pieces of information, if repeated to your teachers, would win the applause they deserve. Here, if you will forgive me, they are a little out of place. A gentleman's knowledge of the ancient authors is not that of a pedant: and I think you have misunderstood the place which philosophy ought to hold in the reasonable life. We do not memorize *systems*. What system can stand? What system does not leave us with the old refrain—*que sais-je?* It is in her power to remind us of the strangeness of things—in the brown charm of her secluded meditations—above all, in her decorative function,—that philosophy becomes instrumental to the good life. We go to the Porch and the Academy to be spectators, not partisans. Drudge! !'

'Dinner is served, sir,' said Drudge, appearing at the door.

Then I dreamed that they went into the dining-room and so to table.

CHAPTER FIVE

Table Talk

THE cowslip wine came with the oysters. It was a little rough, as the old gentleman had prophesied, and the glasses were so very small that Vertue drained his at once. John was afraid that there might be no more to come and therefore dallied over his, partly because he feared that he might put his host out of countenance and partly because he disliked the taste. But his precautions were needless, for with the soup came sherry.

'*Dapibus mensas onerabat inemptis!*' said Mr. Sensible. 'I hope that this wild garden vintage is not unpleasing to an unspoiled palate.'

'You don't mean to say that you have vines?' exclaimed John.

'I was referring to the cowslip wine,' said Mr. Sensible. 'I hope to have some good vines soon, but at present I still rely a little on my neighbours. *Is* this our own sherry, Drudge?'

'No, sir,' said Drudge. 'This is that lot that Mr. Broad sent.'

'Halibut!' said John. 'You surely don't——'

'No,' said Mr. Sensible. 'Sea fish, I confess, I must get from my friends on the coast.'

As the meal went on, John's good manners forbade him to make further inquiries, and when a salad came with one or two very small radishes in it he was positively relieved that his host should be able to claim them as his own produce ('His humble sauce a radish or an egg,' said Mr. Sensible). But in my dream I was privileged to know the sources of the whole meal. The cowslip wine and the radishes were home-grown; the joint had been a present from Mr. Mammon: the entrées and savouries came from Eschropolis: the champagne and ices from old Mr. Halfways. Some of the food was part of the stores which Mr. Sensible had taken over when he came to live there, from his predecessors who had occupied this house before him: for on that tableland, and especially to the North of the main road, the air is so light and cold that things keep for a long time. The bread, the salt, and the apples had been left by Epicurus who was the builder of the house and its first inhabitant. Some very fine hock had belonged to Horace. The claret and also (as I remember) most of the silver, were Montaigne's. But the port, which was one in a thousand and the best thing on that table, had once belonged to Rabelais, who in his turn had it as a present from old Mother Kirk when they were friends. Then I dreamed that after dinner old Mr. Sensible stood up and made a little speech in Latin thanking the Landlord for all they had received.

'What?' said John. 'Do *you* believe in the Landlord?'

'No part of our nature is to be suppressed,' said Mr. Sensible. 'Least of all a part that has enshrined itself in beautiful traditions. The Landlord has his function like everything else as one element in the good life.'

Then presently Mr. Sensible, who was turning very red, fixed his eyes intently on John and repeated.

'As one element. As one element.'

'I see,' said John, and there was a long silence.

'As well,' began Mr. Sensible with great energy some ten minutes later, 'it is part of good manners. Ἀθανάτους μὲν πρῶτα θεούς νόμῳ ὡς διάκειται—Τίμα. My dear Mr. Vertue, my dear young friend, your glass is quite empty. I mean absolutely empty. *Cras ingens iterabimus.*'

There was another and longer pause. John began to wonder whether Mr. Sensible were not asleep, when suddenly Mr. Sensible said with great conviction:

'*Pellite cras ingens tum-tum* νόμῳ ὡς διάκειται.'

Then he smiled at them and finally went to sleep. And presently Drudge came in looking old and thin and dirty in the pale morning light—for I thought that the dawn was just then beginning to show through the chinks of the shutters—to carry his master to bed. Then I saw him come back and lead the guests to their beds. And then the third time I saw him come back into the dining-room and pour out the remains of the claret into a glass and drink it off. Then he stood for a moment or so blinking his red eyes and rubbing his bony, stubbly chin. At last he yawned and set about tidying the room for break-fast.

CHAPTER SIX

Drudge

I DREAMED that John awoke feeling cold. The chamber in which he lay was luxuriously furnished and all the house was silent, so that John thought it would be useless to rise, and he piled all his clothes on him and tried to sleep again. But he only grew colder. Then he said to himself, 'Even if there is no chance of breakfast, I may save myself from

89

freezing by walking about:' so he rose and huddled on all his clothes and went down into the house, but the fires were not yet lit. Finding the back door open he went out. It was full morning of a grey, sunless day. There were dark clouds, fairly low, and as John came out one snowflake fell at his feet, but no more. He found that he was in Mr. Sensible's garden, but it was more of a yard than a garden. A high wall ran all about it and all within the wall was dry, brown earth, with a few stony paths. Dibbling the earth with his foot, John found that the soil was only half an inch deep: under it was solid rock. A little way from the house he found Drudge down on his hands and knees scraping together what seemed to be a little pile of dust, but it was in fact the soil of the garden. The little pile had been got together at the cost of leaving the rock uncovered for a big circle—like a bald patch—all round Drudge.

'Good morning, Drudge,' said John. 'What are you making?'

'Radish beds, sir.'

'Your master is a great gardener.'

'Talks about it, sir.'

'Does he not work in the garden himself?'

'No, sir.'

'It is a poor soil here. Does he manage to feed himself on his own produce in a good year?'

'Feeds me on it, sir.'

'What does the garden grow—besides radishes?'

'Nothing, sir.'

John passed on to the end of the garden and looked over the wall, which was lower here. He drew back with a little start for he found that he was looking down an abyss: the garden was perched on the edge of the Grand Canyon. Below John's feet, at the bottom of the gorge, lay the forest, and on the opposite side he saw a mixture of wood and cliff. The cliffs were all shaggy with trailing and hanging greenery and streams, rendered immovable to sight by their distance, came down from the land beyond. Even on that cold morning the farther side looked richer and warmer than his own.

'We must get out of this,' said John. At that moment Drudge called to him.

'I shouldn't lean on that wall, sir,' he said. 'There's frequent land-slides.'

'Landslides?'

'Yes, sir. I've rebuilt that wall a dozen times. The house used to be right out there—half-way across the gorge.'

'The canyon is getting wider, then?'

'At this point, sir. In Mr. Epicurus' time——'

'You have been employed here under other masters, then?'

'Yes, sir. I've seen a good many of them. Whoever has lived here has always needed me. Choregia they used to call me in the old days, but now they just call me Drudge.'

'Tell me about your old masters,' said John.

'Mr. Epicurus was the first. Mental case he was, poor gentleman: he had a chronic fear of the black hole. Something dreadful. I never had a better employer, though. Nice, kind, quiet-spoken sort of a man. I was very sorry when he went down the cliff——'

'Goodness me!' exclaimed John. 'Do you mean that some of your masters have lost their lives in these landslides?'

'Most of them, sir.'

At that moment a leonine roar came from one of the upper windows of the house.

'Drudge! Son of a bitch! Hot water.'

'Coming, sir,' said Drudge, rising very deliberately from his knees and giving a finishing pat to his heap of dust. 'I shall be leaving here soon,' he continued to John. 'I am thinking of going further North.'

'Further North?'

'Yes, sir. There are openings with Mr. Savage up in the mountains. I was wondering if you and Mr. Vertue were going that way——'

'Drudge!!' bellowed Mr. Sensible's voice from the house.

'Coming, sir,' said Drudge, beginning to untie two pieces of string with which he had confined his trousers beneath his knees. 'So you see, Mr. John, I should be greatly obliged if you would allow me to travel with you.'

'Drudge! Am I to call you again?' shouted Mr. Sensible.

'Coming, sir. If you was to agree I would give Mr. Sensible notice this morning.'

'We are certainly going North for a bit,' said John. 'And I should have no objection, provided Mr. Vertue agrees.'

'Very kind of you, I am sure, sir,' said Drudge. Then he turned and walked slowly into the house.

CHAPTER SEVEN

The Gaucherie of Vertue

MR. SENSIBLE was not in good humour when they met at breakfast. 'That ungrateful blockhead of a servant of mine is leaving me in the lurch,' he said, 'and for the next few days we must shift for ourselves. I fear I am a wretched cook. Perhaps, Vertue, you would indulge me so far as to take the cooking on yourself until I get a new man? I dare say you could enable the three of us to live a very tolerable sort of picnic life for three days?'

The two young men informed him that they were continuing their journey after breakfast.

'This,' said Mr. Sensible, 'is getting really serious. Do you mean to say that you are going to desert me? I am to be reduced to absolute solitude—deprived of the common decencies of life—compelled to spend my day in menial offices? Very well, sir. I am unacquainted with modern manners: no doubt this is the way in which young men now return hospitality.'

'I beg your pardon, sir,' said Vertue. 'I had not seen it in that light. I will certainly act as your servant for a day or so if you wish it. I had not understood that it would be such a burden to you to cook for yourself. I don't remember that you said anything about servants when you were outlining the good life last night.'

'Why, sir,' said Mr. Sensible. 'When I outline the principles of the steam engine I do not explicitly state that I expect fire to burn or the the laws of gravity to operate. There are certain things that one always takes for granted. When I speak of the art of life I presuppose the ordinary conditions of life which that art utilizes.'

'Such as wealth,' said Vertue.

'A competence, a competence,' said Mr. Sensible.

'And health, too?' said Vertue.

'Moderate health,' said Mr. Sensible.

'Your art, then,' said Vertue, 'seems to teach men that the best way of being happy is to enjoy unbroken good fortune in every respect. They would not all find the advice helpful. And now, if Drudge will show me his scullery, I will wash up the breakfast things.'

'You may save yourself the trouble, sir,' said Mr. Sensible drily. 'I cannot pretend to your intensity, and I do not choose to be lectured at the breakfast table. When you have mixed more with the world you will learn not to turn the social board into a schoolroom. In the meantime, forgive me if I feel that I should find your continued society a little fatiguing. Conversation should be like the bee which darts to the next flower before the last has ceased swaying from its airy visit: you make it more like a wood beetle eating its way through a table.'

'As you wish,' said Vertue, 'but how will you do?'

'I shall shut up the house,' said Mr. Sensible, 'and practise αὐτάρκεια in a hotel until I have fitted this place up with such mechanical devices as will henceforth render me wholly independent. I see that I have let myself get behind the times. I should have listened more to certain good friends of mine in the city of Claptrap who have kept abreast of modern invention. They assure me that machinery will soon put the good life beyond the reach of chance: and if mechanism alone will not do it. I know a eugenist who promises to breed us a race of peons who will be psychologically incapable of playing me a trick like this of Drudge's.'

So it fell out that all four left the house together. Mr. Sensible was astonished to find that Drudge (who parted from his employer very civilly) was accompanying the young men. He only shrugged his shoulders, however, and said, '*Vive la bagatelle!* You have stayed in my house which is called Thelema, and its motto is *Do what you will.* So many men, so many minds. I hope I can tolerate anything except intolerance.' Then he went his way and they saw him no more.

BOOK SIX

NORTHWARD ALONG THE CANYON

For being unlike the magnanimous man, they yet ape him; and that in such particulars as they can.—ARISTOTLE

Much of the soul they talk, but all awry,
And in themselves seek virtue.—MILTON

I do not admire the excess of some one virtue unless I am shewn at the same time the excess of the opposite virtue. A man does not prove his greatness by standing at an extremity, but by touching both extremities at once and filling all that lies between them.
—PASCAL

Contempt is a well-recognized defensive reaction.
—I. A. RICHARDS

CHAPTER ONE

First Steps to the North

'IT is of no use keeping to the road,' said Vertue. 'We must explore the cliff-edge as we go along and make trial descents from point to point.'

'Begging your pardon, sir,' said Drudge, 'I know these parts very well and there is no way down, at least within thirty miles. You'll miss nothing by keeping to the road for to-day at any rate.'

'How do you know?' asked Vertue. 'Have you ever tried?'

'Oh, bless you, yes,' said Drudge. 'I've often tried to get across the canyon when I was a youngster.'

'Clearly we had better follow the road,' said John.

'I do not feel quite satisfied,' said Vertue. 'But we can always take the cliffs on the way back. I have an idea that if there is a way down it will be at the extreme north where this gorge opens on the sea: or failing everything, we might manipulate the mouth of the gorge by boat. In the meantime I dare say we might do worse than press on by road.'

'I quite agree,' said John.

Then I saw the three set forward on a more desolate march than I had yet beheld. On every side of them the tableland seemed perfectly flat, but their muscles and lungs soon told them that there was a slight but continuous rise. There was little vegetation—here a shrub, and there some grass: but the most of it was brown earth and moss and rock, and the road beneath them was stone. The grey sky was never broken and I do not remember that they saw a single bird: and it was so bleak that if they stopped at any time to rest, the sweat grew cold on them instantly.

Vertue never abated his pace and Drudge kept even with him though always a respectful yard behind: but I saw that John grew footsore and began to lag. For some hours he was always inventing pretexts to stop and finally he said, 'Friends, it is no use, I can go no further.'

'But you must,' said Vertue.

'The young gentleman is soft, sir, very soft,' said Drudge. 'He is not used to this sort of thing. We'll have to help him along.'

So they took him, one by each arm, and helped him along for a few hours. They found nothing to eat or drink in the waste. Towards evening they heard a desolate voice crying 'Maiwi-maiwi', and looked up, and there was a seagull hanging in the currents of the wind as though it sauntered an invisible stair towards the low rain-clouds.

'Good!' cried Vertue. 'We are nearing the coast.'

'It's a good step yet, sir,' said Drudge. 'These gulls come forty miles inland and more in bad weather.'

Then they plodded on for many more miles. And the sky began to turn from sunless grey to starless black. And they looked and saw a little shanty by the roadside and there they knocked on the door.

CHAPTER TWO

Three Pale Men

WHEN they were let in they found three young men, all very thin and pale, seated by a stove under the low roof of the hut. There was some sacking on a bench along one wall and little comfort else.

'You will fare badly here,' said one of the three men. 'But I am a Steward and it is my duty according to my office to share my supper with you. You may come in.' His name was Mr. Neo-Angular.

'I am sorry that my convictions do not allow me to repeat my friend's offer,' said one of the others. 'But I have had to abandon the humanitarian and egalitarian fallacies.' His name was Mr. Neo-Classical.

'I hope,' said the third, 'that your wanderings in lonely places do not mean that you have any of the romantic virus still in your blood,' His name was Mr. Humanist.

John was too tired and Drudge too respectful to reply: but Vertue said to Mr. Neo-Angular. 'You are very kind. You are saving our lives.'

'I am not kind at all,' said Mr. Neo-Angular with some warmth. 'I am doing my duty. My ethics are based on dogma, not on feeling.'

'I understand you very well,' said Vertue. 'May I shake hands with you?'

'Can it be,' said the other, 'that you are one of us? You are a Catholic? A scholastic?'

'I know nothing about that,' said Vertue, 'but I know that the rule is to be obeyed because it is a rule and not because it appeals to my feelings at the moment.'

'I see you are not one of us,' said Angular, 'and you are undoubtedly damned. *Virtutes paganorum splendida vitia.* Now let us eat.'

Then I dreamed that the three pale men produced three tins of bully beef and six biscuits, and Angular shared his with the guests. There was very little for each and I thought that the best share fell to John and Drudge, for Vertue and the young Steward entered into a kind of rivalry who should leave most for the others.

'Our fare is simple,' said Mr. Neo-Classical. 'And perhaps unwelcome to palates that have been reared on the kickshaws of lower countries. But you see the perfection of form. This beef is a perfect cube: this biscuit a true square.'

'You will admit,' said Mr. Humanist, 'that, at least, our meal is quite free from any lingering flavour of the old romantic sauces.'

'Quite free,' said John, staring at the empty tin.

'It's better than radishes, sir,' said Drudge.

'Do you *live* here, gentlemen?' said Vertue when the empty tins had been removed.

'We do,' said Mr. Humanist. 'We are founding a new community. At present we suffer the hardships of pioneers and have to import our food: but when we have brought the country under cultivation we shall have plenty—as much plenty as is needed for the practice of temperance.'

'You interest me exceedingly,' said Vertue. 'What are the principles of this community?'

'Catholicism, Humanism, Classicism,' said all three.

'Catholicism! Then you are all Stewards?'

'Certainly not,' said Classical and Humanist.

'At least you all believe in the Landlord?'

'I have no interest in the question,' said Classical.

'And I,' said Humanist, 'know perfectly well that the Landlord is a fable.'

'And I,' said Angular, 'know perfectly well that he is a fact.'

'This is very surprising,' said Vertue. 'I do not see how you have come together, or what your common principles can possibly be.'

'We are united by a common antagonism to a common enemy,' said Humanist. 'You must understand that we are three brothers, the sons of old Mr. Enlightenment of the town of Claptrap.'

'I know him,' said John.

'Our father was married twice,' continued Humanist. 'Once to a lady named Epichaerecacia, and afterwards to Euphuia. By his first wife he had a son called Sigmund who is thus our step-brother.'

'I know him too,' said John.

'We are the children of his second marriage,' said Humanist.

'Then,' cried Vertue, 'we are related—if you care to acknowledge the kinship. You have probably heard that Euphuia had a child before she married your father. I was that child—though I confess that I never discovered who my father was and enemies have hinted that I am a bastard.'

'You have said quite sufficient,' replied Angular. 'You can hardly expect that the subject should be agreeable to us. I might add that my office, if there were nothing else, sets me apart even from my legitimate relations.'

'And what about the common antagonism?' said John.

'We were all brought up,' said Humanist, 'by our step-brother in the university at Eschropolis, and we learned there to see that whoever stays with Mr. Halfways must either come on to Eschropolis or else remain at Thrill as the perpetual minion of his brown daughter.'

'You had not been with Mr. Halfways yourselves, then?' asked John.

'Certainly not. We learned to hate him from watching the effect which his music had on other people. Hatred of him is the first thing that unites us. Next, we discovered how residence in Eschropolis inevitably leads to the giant's dungeon.'

'I know all about that too,' said John.

'Our common hatred therefore links us together against the giant, against Eschropolis, and against Mr. Halfways.'

'But specially against the latter,' said Classical.

'I should rather say,' remarked Angular, 'against half-measures and

99

compromises of all sorts—against any pretence that there is any kind of goodness or decency, any even tolerable temporary resting-place, on this side of the Grand Canyon.'

'And that,' said Classical, 'is why Angular is for me, in one sense, *the* enemy, but, in another, *the* friend. I cannot agree with his notions about the other side of the canyon: but just because he relegates his delusions to the *other* side, he is free to agree with me about this side and to be an implacable exposer (like myself) of all attempts to foist upon us any transcendental, romantical, optimistic trash.'

'My own feeling,' said Humanist, 'is rather that Angular is with me in guarding against any confusion of the *levels* of experience. He *canalizes* all the mystical nonsense—the *sehnsucht* and *Wanderlust* and Nympholepsy—and transfers them to the far side: that prevents their drifting about on this side and hindering our real function. It leaves us free to establish a really tolerable and even comfortable civilization here on the plateau; a culture based alike on those truths which Mr. Sensible acknowledges and on those which the giant reveals, but throwing over both alike a graceful veil of illusion. And that way we shall remain human: we shall not become beasts with the giant nor abortive angels with Mr. Halfways.'

'The young gentleman is asleep, sir,' said Drudge: and indeed John had sunk down some time ago.

'You must excuse him,' said Vertue. 'He found the road long to-day.'

Then I saw that all six men lay down together in the sacking. The night was far colder than the night they passed in Mr. Sensible's house: but as there was here no pretence of comfort and they lay huddled together in the narrow hut, John slept warmer here than at Thelema.

CHAPTER THREE

Neo-Angular

WHEN they rose in the morning John was so footsore and his limbs ached so that he knew not how to continue his journey. Drudge assured them that the coast could not now be very far. He thought that Vertue could reach it and return in a day and that John might await him in the hut. As for John himself, he was loth to burden hosts who lived in such apparent poverty: but Mr. Angular constrained him to stay, when he had explained that the secular virtue of hospitality was worthless, and care for the afflicted a sin if it proceeded from humanitarian sentiment, but that he was obliged to act as he did by the rules of his order. So, in my dream, I saw Drudge and Vertue set out northwards alone, while John remained with the three pale men.

In the forenoon he had a conversation with Angular.

'You believe, then,' said John, 'that there is a way across the canyon?'

'I know there is. If you will let me take you to Mother Kirk she will carry you over in a moment.'

'And yet, I am not sure that I am not sailing under false colours. When I set out from home, crossing the canyon was never in my thoughts—still less was Mother Kirk.'

'It does not matter in the least what was in your thoughts.'

'It does, to me. You see, my only motive for crossing, is the hope that something I am looking for may be on the other side.'

'That is a dangerous, subjective motive. What is this something?'

'I saw an Island——'

'Then you must forget it as soon as you can. Islands are the Halfways' concern. I assure you, you must eradicate every trace of that nonsense from your mind before I can help you.'

'But how can you help me after removing the only thing that I want to be helped to? What is the use of telling a hungry man that you will grant him his desires, provided there is no question of eating?'

'If you do not *want* to cross the canyon, there is no more to be said. But, then, you must realize where you are. Go on with your Island, if you like, but do not pretend that it is anything but a part of the land of destruction this side of the canyon. If you are a sinner, for heaven's sake have the grace to be a cynic too.'

'But how can you say that the Island is all bad, when it is longing for the Island, and nothing else, that has brought me this far?'

'It makes no difference. All on this side of the canyon is much of a muchness. If you confine yourself to this side, then the Spirit of the Age is right.'

'But this is not what Mother Kirk said. She particularly insisted that some of the food was much less poisonous than the rest.'

'So you have met Mother Kirk? No wonder that you are confused. You had no business to talk to her except through a qualified Steward. Depend upon it, you have misunderstood every word she said.'

'Then there was Reason, too. She refused to say that the Island was an illusion. But perhaps, like Mr. Sensible, you have quarrelled with Reason.'

'Reason is divine. But how should you understand her? You are a beginner. For you, the only safe commerce with Reason is to learn from your superiors the dogmata in which her deliverances have been codi-fied for general use.'

'Look here,' said John. 'Have you ever seen my Island?'

'God forbid.'

'And you have never heard Mr. Halfways either.'

'Never. And I never will. Do you take me for an escapist?'

'Then there is at least one object in the world of which I know more than you. I have *tasted* what you call romantic trash; you have only talked about it. You need not tell me that there is a danger in it and an element of evil. Do you suppose that I have not felt that danger and that evil a thousand times more than you? But I know also that the evil in it is not what I went to it to find, and that I should have sought nothing and found nothing without it. I know this by experience as I know a dozen things about it which of you betray your ignorance as often as you speak. Forgive me if I am rude: but how is it possible that you can advise me in this matter? Would you recommend a eunuch as confes-sor to a man whose difficulties lay in the realm of chastity? Would a man born blind be my best guide against the lust of the eye? But I am getting angry. And you have shared your biscuit with me. I ask your pardon.'

'It is part of my office to bear insults with patience,' said Mr. Angu-lar.

CHAPTER FOUR

Humanist

IN the afternoon Mr. Humanist took John out to show him the garden, by whose produce, in time, the new culture was to become self-supporting. As there was no human, or indeed animal, habitation within sight, no wall or fence had been deemed necessary, but the area of the garden had been marked out by a line of stones and sea-shells alternately arranged: and this was necessary as the garden would else have been indistinguishable from the waste. A few paths, also marked by stones and shells, were arranged in a geometrical pattern.

'You see,' said Mr. Humanist, 'we have quite abandoned the ideas of the old romantic landscape gardeners. You notice a certain severity. A landscape gardener would have had a nodding grove over there on the right, and a mound on the left, and winding paths, and a pond, and flower-beds. He would have filled the obscurer parts with the means of sensuality—the formless potato and the romantically irregular cabbage. You see, there is nothing of the sort here.'

'Nothing at all,' said John.

'At present, of course, it is not very fruitful. But we are pioneers.'

'Do you ever try *digging* it?' suggested John.

'Why, no,' said Mr. Humanist, 'you see, it is pure rock an inch below the surface, so we do not disturb the soil. That would remove the graceful veil of illusion which is so necessary to the *human* point of view.'

CHAPTER FIVE

Food from the North

LATE that evening the door of the hut opened and Vertue staggered in and dropped to a sitting position by the stove. He was very exhausted and it was long before he had his breath to talk. When he had, his first words were:

'You must leave this place, gentlemen. It is in danger.'

'Where is Drudge?' said John.

'He stayed there.'

'And what is this danger?' asked Mr. Humanist.

'I'm going to tell you. By the by, there's no way over the gorge northward.'

'We have been on a fool's errand, then,' said John, 'ever since we left the main road.'

'Except that now we know,' replied Vertue. 'But I must eat before I can tell my story. To-night I am able to return our friends' hospitality, and with that he produced from various parts of his clothing the remains of a handsome cold pie, two bottles of strong beer and a little flask of rum. For some time there was silence in the hut, and when the meal was finished and a little water had been boiled so that each had a glass of hot grog, Vertue began his story.

CHAPTER SIX

Furthest North

'IT is all like this as far as the mountains—about fifteen miles—and there is nothing to tell of our journey except rock and moss and a few gulls. The mountains are frightful as you approach them, but the road runs up to a pass and we had not much difficulty. Beyond the pass you get into a little rocky valley and it was here that we first found any signs of habitation. The valley is a regular warren of caves inhabited by dwarfs. There are several species of them, I gather, though I only distinguished two—a black kind with black shirts and a red kind who call themselves Marxomanni. They are all very fierce and apparently quarrel a good deal but they all acknowledge some kind of vassalage to this man Savage. At least they made no difficulty in letting me through when they heard that I wanted to see him—beyond insisting on giving me a guard. It was there I lost Drudge. He said he had come to join the red dwarfs and would I mind going on alone. He was just the same up to the end—civil as ever—but he was down one of their burrows and apparently quite at home before I could get in a word. Then my dwarfs took me on. I didn't care for the arrangements much. They were not men, you know, not dwarf men, but real dwarfs— trolls. They could talk, and they walk on two legs, but the structure must be quite different from ours. I felt all the time that if they killed me it wouldn't be murder, any more than if a crocodile or a gorilla killed me. It *is* a different species—however it came there. Different faces.

'Well, they kept taking me up and up. It was all rocky zig-zags, round and round. Fortunately, I do not get giddy. My chief danger was the wind whenever we got on a ridge—for of course my guides, being only some three feet high, did not offer it the same target. I had one or two narrow escapes. Savage's nest is a terrifying place. It is a long hall like a barn and when I first caught sight of it—half-way up the sky from where they were leading me—I thought to myself that wherever else we were going it could not be *there*; it looked so inacces-sible. But on we went.

'One thing you must get into your heads is that there are caves all the way up, all inhabited. The whole mountain must be honeycombed. I saw thousands of the dwarfs. Like an ant-hill—and not a man in the place except me.

'From Savage's nest you look straight down to the sea. I should think it is the biggest sheer drop on any coast. It was from there that I saw the mouth of the gorge. The mouth is only a lowering of the cliff: from the lowest part of the opening it is still thousands of feet to the sea. There is no conceivable landing. It is no use to anyone but sea-gulls.

'But you want to hear about Savage. He sat on a high chair at the end of his barn—a very big man, almost a giant. When I say that I don't mean his height: I had the same feeling about him that I had about the dwarfs. That doubt about the *species*. He was dressed in skins and had an iron helmet on his head with horns stuck in it.

'He had a woman there, too, a great big woman with yellow hair and high cheek-bones. Grimhild her name is. And the funny thing is that she is the sister of an old friend of yours, John. She is Mr. Halfways' elder daughter. Apparently Savage came down to Thrill and carried her off: and what is stranger still, both the girl and the old gentleman were rather pleased about it than otherwise.

'As soon as the dwarfs brought me in, Savage rapped on the table and bellowed out, "Lay the board for us men," and she set about laying it. He didn't say anything to me for a long time. He just sat and looked and sang. He had only one song and he was singing it off and on all the time I was there. I remember bits of it.

'Wind age, wolf age,
Ere the world crumbles:
Shard age, spear age,
Shields are broken. . . .

'Then there was another bit began:

'East sits the Old 'Un
In Iron-forest;
Feeds amidst it
Fenris' children. . . .

I sat down after a bit, for I did not want him to think I was afraid of him. When the food was on the table he asked me to have some, so I had it. He offered me a sweet drink, very strong, in a horn, so I drank it. Then he shouted and drank himself and said that mead in a horn was all he could offer me at present: "But soon," he said, "I shall drink the blood of men from skulls." There was a lot of this sort of stuff. We ate roast pork, with our fingers. He kept on singing his song and shouting. It was only after dinner that he began to talk connectedly. I wish I could remember it all. This is the important part of my story.

'It is hard to understand it without being a biologist. These dwarfs *are* a different species and an older species than ours. But, then, the specific variation is always liable to reappear in human children. They revert to the dwarf. Consequently, they are multiplying very fast; they are being increased both by ordinary breeding among themselves and also from without by those hark-backs or changelings. He spoke of lots of sub-species besides the Marxomanni—Mussolimini, Swastici,

Gangomanni. . . . I can't remember them all. For a long time I couldn't see where he himself came in.

'At last he told me. He is breeding and training them for a descent on this country. When I tried to find out why, for a long time he would only stare at me and sing his song. Finally—as near as as I could get it—his theory seemed to be that fighting was an end in itself.

'Mind you, he was not drunk. He said that he could understand old-fashioned people who believed in the Landlord and kept the rules and hoped to go up and live in the Landlord's castle when they had to leave this country. "They have something to live for," he said. "And if their belief was true, their behaviour would be perfectly sensible. But as their belief is not true, there remains only one way of life fit for a man." This other way of life was something he called Heroism, or Master-Morality, or Violence. "All the other people in between," he said, "are ploughing the sand." He went on railing at the people in Claptrap for ages, and also at Mr. Sensible. "These are the dregs of man," he said. "They are always thinking of happiness. They are scraping together and storing up and trying to *build*. Can they not see that the law of the world is against them? Where will any of them be a hundred years hence?" I said they might be building for posterity. "And who will posterity build for?" he asked. "Can't you see that it is all bound to come to nothing in the end? And the end may come to-morrow: and however late it comes, to those who look back all their 'happiness' will seem but a moment that has slipped away and left nothing behind. You can't gather happiness. Do you go to bed with any more in hand on the day you have had a thousand pleasures?" I asked if his "Heroism" left anything behind it either: but he said it did. "The excellent deed," he said, "is eternal. The hero alone has this privilege, that death for him is not defeat, and the lamenting over him and the memory is part of the good he aimed for; and the moment of battle fears nothing from the future because it has already cast security away."

'He talked a lot like that. I asked him what he thought of the Eschropolitans and he roared with laughter and said: "When the Cruels meet the Clevers there will not be even the ghost of a tug of war." Then I asked him if he knew you three and he laughed louder

107

still. He said that Angular might turn out an enemy worth fighting when he grew up. "But I don't know," he said. "Likely enough he is only an Eschropolitan turned inside-out—poacher turned game-keeper. As for the other pair, they are the last even of the last men." I asked him what he meant. "The men of Claptrap," he said, "may have some excuse for their folly, for they at least still believe that your country is a place where Happiness is possible. But your two friends are madmen without qualification. They claim to have reached rock-bottom, they talk of being disillusioned. They think that they have reached the furthest North—as if I were not here to the North of them. They live on a rock that will never feed man, between a chasm that they cannot cross and the home of a giant to whom they dare not return: and still they maunder of a culture and a security. If all men who try to build are but polishing the brasses on a sinking ship, then your pale friends are the supreme fools who polish with the rest though they know and admit that the ship is sinking. Their Humanism and what not is but the old dream with a new name. The rot in the world is too deep and the leak in the world is too wide. They may patch and tinker as they please, they will not save it. Better give in. Better cut the wood with the grain. If I am to live in a world of destruction let me be its agent and not its patient."

'In the end he said: "I will make this concession to your friends. They do live further North than anyone but me. They are more like men than any of their race. They shall have this honour when I lead the dwarfs to war, that Humanist's skull shall be the first from which I drink the blood of a man: and Grimhild here shall have Classical's."

'That was about all he said. He made me go out on the cliffs with him. It was all I could do to keep my footing. He said, "This wind blows straight from the pole; it will make a man of you." I think he was trying to frighten me. In the end I got away. He loaded me with food for myself and you. "Feed them up," he said. "There is not enough blood in them at present to quench the thirst of a dwarfish sword." Then I came away. And I am very tired.'

CHAPTER SEVEN

Fools' Paradise

'I SHOULD like to meet this Savage,' said Angular. 'He seems to be a very clear-headed man.'

'I don't know about that,' said Humanist. 'He and his dwarfs seem to me to be just the thing I am fighting against—the logical conclusion of Eschropolis against which I raise the banner of Humanism. All the wild atavistic emotions which old Halfways sets free under false pretences—I am not at all surprised that he likes a valkyrie for a daughter —and which young Halfways unmasks, but cherishes when he has unmasked them; where can they end but in a complete abandonment of the *human*? I am glad to hear of him. He shows how necessary I am.'

'I agree,' said John in great excitement, 'But how are you going to fight? Where are your troops? Where is your base of supplies? You can't feed an army on a garden of stones and sea-shells.'

'It is intelligence that counts,' said Humanist.

'It moves nothing,' said John. 'You see that Savage is scalding hot and you are cold. You must get heat to rival his heat. Do you think you can rout a million armed dwarfs by being "not romantic"?'

'If Mr. Vertue will not be offended,' said Classical, 'I would suggest that he dreamed the whole thing. Mr. Vertue is romantic: he is paying for his wish-fulfilment dreams as he will always pay—with a fear-fulfilment dream. It is well-known that nobody lives further North than we.' But Vertue was too tired to defend his story and soon all the occupants of the hut were asleep.

BOOK SEVEN

SOUTHWARD ALONG THE CANYON

Now is the seventh winter since Troy fell, and we
Still search beneath unfriendly stars, through every sea
And desert isle, for Italy's retreating strand.
But here is kinsman's country and Acestes' land;
What hinders here to build a city and remain?
Oh fatherland, oh household spirits preserved in vain
From the enemy, shall no new Troy arise? Shall no
New Simois there, re-named for Hector's memory, flow?
Rather, come!—burn with me the boats that work us harm!
                                                    —VIRGIL

Through this and through no other fault we fell,
Nor, being fallen, bear other pain than this,
—Always without hope in desire to dwell.—DANTE

Some also have wished that the next way to their Father's house were here that they
might be troubled no more with either Hills or Mountains to go over; but the way is the
way, and there's an end.—BUNYAN

CHAPTER ONE

Vertue is Sick

I SAW the two travellers get up from their sacking and bid good-bye to their hosts, and set out southwards. The weather had not changed, nor did I ever see any other weather over that part of the country than clouds and wind without rain. Vertue himself was out of sorts and made haste without the spirit of haste. Then at last he opened his mind to his companion and said, 'John, I do not know what is coming over me. Long ago you asked me—or was it Media asked me—where I was going and why: and I remember that I brushed the question aside. At that time it seemed to me so much more important to keep my·rules and do my thirty miles a day. But I am beginning to find that it will not do. In the old days it was always a question of doing what I chose instead of what I wanted: but now I am beginning to be uncertain what it is I choose.'

'How has this come about?' said John.

'Do you know that I nearly decided to stay with Savage?'

'With Savage?'

'It sounds like raving, but think it over. Supposing there is no Landlord, no mountains in the East, no Island in the West, nothing but this country. A few weeks ago I would have said that all those things made no difference. But now—I don't know. It is quite clear that all the ordinary ways of living in this country lead to something which I certainly do *not* choose. I know that, even if I don't know what I *do* choose. I know that I don't want to be a Halfways, or a Clever, or a Sensible. Then there is the life I have been leading myself—marching on I don't know where. I can't see that there is any other good in it except the mere fact of imposing my will on my inclinations. And that seems to be good *training,* but training for what? Suppose after all it was training for battle? Is it so absurd to think that that might be the thing we were born for? A fight in a narrow place, life or death;—that must be the final act of will—the conquest of the deepest inclination of all.'

'I think my heart will break,' said John after they had gone many paces in silence. 'I came out to find my Island. I am not high-minded like you, Vertue: it was never anything but sweet desire that led me. I have not smelled the air from that Island since—since—it is so long that I cannot remember. I saw more of it at home. And now my only friend talks of selling himself to the dwarfs.'

'I am sorry for you,' said Vertue, 'and I am sorry for myself. I am sorry for every blade of grass and for this barren rock we are treading and the very sky above us. But I have no help to give you.'

'Perhaps,' said John, 'there are things East and West of this country after all.'

'Do you still understand me so little as that!' cried Vertue, turning on him. 'Things East and West! Don't you see that that is the other fatal possibility? Don't you see that I am caught either way?'

'Why?' said John: and then, 'Let us sit down. I am tired and we have nowhere to hurry to—not now.'

Vertue sat down as one not noticing that he did it.

'Don't you see?' he said. 'Suppose there is anything East and West. How can that give me a motive for going on? Because there is something pleasant ahead? That is a bribe. Because there is something dreadful behind? That is a threat. I meant to be a free man. I meant to choose things because I chose to choose them—not because I was paid for it. Do you think I am a child to be scared with rods and baited with sugar plums? It was for this reason that I never even inquired whether the stories about the Landlord were true; I saw that his castle and his black hole were there to corrupt my will and kill my freedom. It it was true it was a truth an honest man must not know.' ‑

Evening darkened on the tableland and they sat for a long time, immovable.

'I believe that I am mad,' said Vertue presently. 'The world cannot be as it seems to me. If there is something to go to, it is a bribe, and I cannot go to it: if I can go, then there is nothing to go to.'

'Vertue,' said John, 'give in. For once yield to desire. Have done with your choosing. *Want* something.'

'I cannot,' said Vertue. 'I must choose because I choose because I choose: and it goes on for ever, and in the whole world I cannot find a reason for rising from this stone.'

'Is it not reason enough that the cold will presently kill us here?'

It had grown quite dark, and Vertue made no reply.

'Vertue!' said John, and then suddenly again in a louder voice, frightened, 'Vertue!!' But there was no answer. He groped for his friend in the dark and touched the cold dust of the tableland. He rose on his hands and knees and groped all about, calling. But he was confused and could not even find again the place whence he had risen himself. He could not tell how often he might have groped over the same ground or whether he was getting further and further from their resting-place. He could not be still; it was too cold. So all that night he rummaged to and fro in the dark, calling out Vertue's name: and often it came into his head that Vertue had been all along one of the phantoms of a dream and that he had followed a shade.

CHAPTER TWO

John Leading

I DREAMED that morning broke over the plateau, and I saw John rise up, white and dirty, in the new twilight. He looked all round him and saw nothing but the heath. Then he walked this way and that, still looking, and so for a long time. And at last he sat down and wept: that also for a long time. And when he had wept enough he rose like a man determined and resumed his journey southward.

He had hardly gone twenty paces when he stopped with a cry, for there lay Vertue at his feet. I understood in my dream that during his groping in the darkness he had unwittingly gone further and further from the place where they had first sat down.

In a moment John was on his knees and feeling for Vertue's heart. It beat still. He laid his face to Vertue's lips. They breathed still. He caught him by the shoulder and shook him.

'Wake up,' he cried, 'the morning is here.'

Then Vertue opened his eyes and smiled at John, a little foolishly.

'Are you well?' said John. 'Are you fit to travel?'

But Vertue only smiled. He was dumb. Then John held out his

hands and pulled Vertue to his feet: and Vertue stood up uncertainly, but as soon as he made a stride he stumbled and fell, for he was blind. It was long before John understood. Then at last I saw him take Vertue by the hand and, leading him, resume their journey to the South. And there fell upon John that last loneliness which comes when the comforter himself needs comforting, and the guide is to be guided.

CHAPTER THREE

The Main Road Again

THEY found Mr. Sensible's house empty, as John had expected, with the shutters up and the chimneys smokeless. John decided to push on to the main road and then, if the worst came to the worst, they could go to Mother Kirk: but he hoped it would not come to that.

All their journey South had been a descent, from the northern mountains to Mr. Sensible's: but after his house it began to rise again a little to the main road, which ran along a low ridge, so that, when they had gained the road, the country South of it was suddenly all opened before them. At the same moment there came a gleam of sunshine, the first for many days. The road was unfenced to the heath on its northern side, but in its southern side there was a hedge with a gate in it: and the first thing John saw through the gate was a long low mound of earth. He had not been a farmer's son for nothing. Having led Vertue to the bank of the road and seated him, he lost no time in climbing the gate and digging with both hands into the earthern mound. It contained, as he had expected, turnips; and in a minute he was seated by Vertue, cutting a fine root into chunks, feeding the blind man and teaching him how to feed himself. The sun grew warmer every moment. The spring seemed further on in this place, and the hedge behind them was already more green than brown. Among many notes of birds John thought he could distinguish a lark. They had breakfasted well, and as the warmth increased pleasantly over their aching limbs, they fell asleep.

115

CHAPTER FOUR

Going South

WHEN John awoke his first look was towards Vertue, but Vertue was still sleeping. John stretched himself and rose: he was warm and well, but a little thirsty. It was a four-cross-road where they had been sitting, for the northern road, at which John looked with a shudder, was but the continuation of a road from the South. He stood and looked down the latter. To his eyes, long now accustomed to the dusty flats of the northern plateau, the country southward was as a rich counterpane. The sun had passed noon by an hour or so, and the slanting light freckled with rounded shadows a green land, that fell ever away before him, opening as it sank into valleys, and beyond then into deeper valleys again, so that places on the same level where now he stood, yonder were mountain tops. Nearer hand were fields and hedgerows, ruddy ploughland, winding woods, and frequent farm-houses white among their trees. He went back and raised Vertue and was about to show it all to him when he remembered his blindness. Then, sighing, he took him by the hand and went down the new road.

Before they had gone far he heard a bubbling sound by the roadside, and found a little spring pouring itself into a stream that ran henceforth with the road, now at the left, now at the right, and often crossed their way. He filled his hat with water and gave Vertue to drink. Then he drank himself and they went on, always downhill. The road nestled deeper each half-mile between banks of grass. There were primroses, first one or two, then clustered, then innumerable. From many turns of the road John caught sight of the deeper valleys to which they were descending, blue with distance and rounded with the weight of trees: but often a little wood cut off all remoter prospect.

The first house they came to was a red house, old and ivied, and well back from the road, and John thought it had the look of a Steward's house: as they came nearer, there was the Steward himself, without his mask, pottering about at some light gardening labour on the sunny side of the hedge. John leaned over the gate and asked for hospitality, explaining at the same time his friend's condition.

'Come in, come in,' said the Steward. 'It will be a great pleasure.'

Now I dreamed that this Steward was the same Mr. Broad who had sent a case of sherry to Mr. Sensible. He was about sixty years of age.

CHAPTER FIVE

Tea on the Lawn

'IT is almost warm enough to have tea on the lawn,' said Mr. Broad. 'Martha, I think we will have tea on the lawn.'

Chairs were set and all three sat down. On the smooth lawn, surrounded by laurels and laburnum, it was even warmer than in the road, and suddenly a sweet bird-note shot out from the thickets.

'Listen!' said Mr. Broad, 'it is a thrush. I really believe it is a thrush.'

Maidservants in snowy aprons opened the long windows of the library and came over the grass carrying tables and trays, the silver teapot and the stand of cakes. There was honey for tea. Mr. Broad asked John some questions about his travels.

'Dear me,' he said, when he heard of Mr. Savage, 'dear me! I ought to go and see him. And such a clever man, too, by your account . . . it is very sad.'

John went on to describe the three pale men.

'Ah, to be sure,' said Mr. Broad. 'I knew their father very well. A very able man. I owed a good deal to him at one time. Indeed, as a young man, he formed my mind, I suppose I ought to go and see his boys. Young Angular I *have* met. He is a dear, good fellow—a little narrow; I would venture to say, even a little old-fashioned, though of course I wouldn't for the world—the two brothers are doing splendidly I have no doubt. I really *ought* to go and see them. But I am getting on, and I confess it never suits me up there.'

'It is a very different climate from this,' said John.

'I always think it is possible for a place to be *too* bracing. They call it the land of the Tough-minded—tough-skinned would be a better name. If one has a tendency to lumbago—But, dear me, if you have come from there you must have met my old friend Sensible?'

'You know him too?'

'Know him? He is my oldest friend. He is a kind of connection of mine, and then, you know, we are quite near neighbours. He is only a mile north of the road and I am about a mile south of it. I should think I did know him. I have passed many, many happy hours in his house. The dear old man. Poor Sensible, he is ageing fast. I don't think he has ever quite forgiven me for having kept most of my hair!'

'I should have thought his views differed from yours a good deal.'

'Ah, to be sure, to be sure! He is not very orthodox, perhaps, but as I grow older I am inclined to set less and less store by mere orthodoxy. So often the orthodox view means the lifeless view, the barren formula. I am coming to look more and more at the language of the heart. Logic and definition divide us: it is those things which draw us together that I now value most—our common affections, our common delight in this slow pageant of the countryside, our common struggle towards the light. Sensible's heart is in the right place.'

'I wonder,' said John, 'if he treats that servant of his very well.'

'His language is a little bit rough, I suppose. One must be charitable. You young people are so hard. Dear me, I remember when I was a boy myself. . . . And then a man of Sensible's age suffers a good deal. We are none of us perfect. Will you not have a little more tea?'

'Thank you,' said John, 'but if you can give me some directions I think I would like to continue my journey. I am trying to find an Island in the West——'

'That is a beautiful idea,' said Mr. Broad. 'And if you will trust an older traveller, the seeking is the finding. How many happy days you have before you!'

'And I want to know,' continued John, 'whether it is really necessary to cross the canyon.'

'To be sure you do. I wouldn't for the world hold you back. At the same time, my dear boy, I think there is a very real danger at your age of trying to make these things too definite. That has been the great error of my profession in past ages. We have tried to enclose everything in formulæ, to turn poetry into logic, and metaphor into dogma; and now that we are beginning to realize our mistake we find ourselves shackled by the formulæ of dead men. I don't say that they were not adequate once: but they have ceased to be adequate for us with our wider know-ledge. When I became a man, I put away childish things. These great truths need re-interpretation in every age.'

'I am not sure that I quite understand,' said John. 'Do you mean that I must cross the canyon or that I must not?'

'I see you want to pin me down,' said Mr. Broad, with a smile, 'and I love to see it. I was like that myself once. But one loses faith in abstract logic as one grows older. Do you never feel that the truth is so great and so simple that no mere words can contain it? The heaven and the heaven of heavens . . . how much less this house that I have builded.'

'Well, anyway,' said John, deciding to try a new question. 'Suppos-ing a man *did* have to cross the canyon. Is it true that he would have to rely on Mother Kirk?'

'Ah, Mother Kirk! I love and honour her from the bottom of my heart, but I trust that loving her does not mean being blind to her faults. We are none of us infallible. If I sometimes feel that I must differ from her at present, it is because I honour all the more the *idea* that she stands for, the thing she may yet become. For the moment, there is no denying that she has let herself get a little out of date. Surely, for many of our generation, there is a truer, a more acceptable, message in all this beautiful world around us? I don't know whether you are anything of a botanist. If you would care——'

'I want my Island,' said John. 'Can you tell me how to reach it? I am afraid I am not specially interested in botany.'

'It would open a new world to you,' said Mr. Broad. 'A new window on the Infinite. But perhaps this is not in your line. We must all find our own key to the mystery after all. I wouldn't for the world . . .'

'I think I must be going,' said John. 'And I have enjoyed myself very much. If I follow this road, shall I find anywhere that will give me a night's lodging in a few miles?'

'Oh, easily,' said Mr. Broad. 'I should be very glad to have you here if you would care to stay. But if not, there is Mr. Wisdom within an easy walk. You will find him a delightful man. I used to go and see him quite often when I was younger, but it is a little too far for me now. A dear, good fellow—a *little* persistent, perhaps . . . I sometimes wonder if he is really quite free from a trace of narrow-mindedness. . . . You should hear what Sensible says about him! But there: we are none of us perfect, and he is a very good sort of man on the whole. You will like him very much.'

The old Steward bade good-bye to John with almost fatherly kindness, and John, still leading Vertue, pursued his journey.

CHAPTER SIX

The House of Wisdom

THE stream that they had followed to the Steward's house was now no longer a brook by the roadside, but a river that sometimes approached, sometimes receded from the road, sliding in swift amber reaches and descending silver rapids. The trees grew more thickly hereabouts and were of larger kinds—and as the valley deepened, tiers of forest rose one above the other on each side. They walked in shadow. But far above their heads the sun was still shining on the mountain tops, beyond the forest slopes and beyond the last steep fields, where there were domed summits of pale grass and winding water-glens, and cliffs the colour of doves, and cliffs the colour of wine. The moths were already flying when they reached an open place. The valley widened and a loop of the river made room for a wide and level lawn between its banks and the wooded mountains. Amidst the lawn stood a low, pillared house approachable by a bridge, and the door stood open. John led the sick man up to them and saw that the lamps were already lit within; and then he saw Wisdom sitting among his children, like an old man.

'You may stay here as long as you wish,' he said in answer to John's question. 'And it may be that we shall heal your friend if his sickness is not incurable. Sit and eat, and when you have eaten you shall tell us your story.'

Then I saw that chairs were brought for the travellers and some of the young men of the house carried water to them to wash. And when they had washed, a woman set a table before them and laid on it a loaf, and cheese, and a dish of fruit, with some curds, and butter-milk in a pitcher: 'For we can get no wine here,' said the old man with a sigh.

When the meal was over there was silence in the house, and John saw that they waited for his story. So he collected himself and cast back in his mind, a long time, in silence; and when at last he spoke he told the whole thing in order, from the first sight he had had of the Island down to his arrival among them.

Then Vertue was led away from John, and he himself was brought into a cell where there was a bed, and a table, and a pitcher of water. He lay on the bed, and it was hard, but not lumpy, and he was immediately in a deep sleep.

CHAPTER SEVEN

Across the Canyon by Moonlight

IN the middle of the night he opened his eyes and saw the full moon, very large and low, shining at his window: and beside his bed stood a woman darkly clothed, who held up her hand for silence when he would have spoken.

'My name is Contemplation,' she said, 'and I am one of the daughters of Wisdom. You must rise and follow me.'

Then John rose and followed her out of the house on to the grassy lawn in the moonlight. She led him across it to its westward edge where the mountain began to rise under its cloak of forest. But as they came right up to the eaves of the forest he saw that there was a crack or crevasse in the earth between them and it, to which he could find no bottom, and though it was not very wide, it was too wide to jump.

'It is too wide a jump by day,' said the lady, 'but in the moonlight you can jump it.'

John felt no doubt of her and gathered himself together and leaped. His leap carried him further than he had intended—though he felt no surprise—and he found himself flying over the tree tops and the steep fields, and he never alighted till he reached the mountain top; and the Lady was there by his side.

'Come,' she said, 'we have still far to go.'

Then they went on together over hills and dales, very fast, in the moonlight, till they came to the edge of a cliff, and he looked down and saw the sea below him: and out in the sea lay the Island. And because it was moonlight and night John could not see it so well as he had sometimes seen it, but either for that reason, or for some other, it seemed to him the more real.

'When you have learned to fly further, we can leap from here right into the Island,' said the Lady. 'But for this night, it is enough.'

As John turned to answer her, the Island and the sea and the Lady herself vanished, and he was awake, in daylight, in his cell in the house of Wisdom, and a bell was ringing.

CHAPTER EIGHT

This Side by Sunlight

ON the next day Mr. Wisdom caused John and Vertue both to sit by him in a porch of his house looking westward. The wind was in the South and the sky was a little clouded and over the western mountains there was a delicate mist, so that they had the air of being in another world, though they were not more than a mile away. And Mr. Wisdom instructed them.

'As to this Island in the West, and those eastern mountains, and as touching the Landlord also and the Enemy, there are two errors, my sons, which you must equally conquer, and pass right between them, before you can become wise. The first error is that of the southern people, and it consists in holding that these eastern and western places are real places—real as this valley is real, and places as this valley is a place. If any such thought lingers in your minds, I would have you root it out utterly, and give no quarter to that thought, whether it threatens you with fears, or tempts you with hopes. For this is Supersti⁄

tion, and all who believe it will come in the end to the swamps and the jungles of the far South, where they will live in the city of Magicians, transported with delight in things that help not, and haunted with terror of that which cannot hurt. And it is part of the same error to think that the Landlord is a real man: real as I am real, man as I am man. That is the first error. And the second is the opposite of it, and is chiefly current to the North of the road: it is the error of those who say that the eastern and western things are merely illusions in our own minds. This also it is my will that you should utterly reject: and you must be on your guard lest you ever embrace this error in your fear of the other, or run to and fro between the two as your hearts will prompt you to do, like some who will be Materialists (for that is the name of the second error) when the story of the black hole frightens them for their lawless living, or even when they are afraid of spectres, and then another day will believe in the Landlord and the castle because things in this country go hard with them, or because the lease of some dear friend is running out and they would gladly hope to meet him again. But the wise man, ruling his passions with reason and disciplined imagination, withdraws himself to the middle point between these two errors, having found that the truth lies there, and remains fixed immovably. But what that truth is you shall learn to-morrow; and for the present this sick man will be cared for, and you who are whole may do as you will.'

Then I saw Mr. Wisdom rise and leave them, and Vertue was taken to another place. John spent the most part of that day walking in the neighbourhood of the house. He crossed the level grass of the valley and came to its western edge where the mountain began to rise under its cloak of forest. But as he came under the forest eaves, he saw that between him and the first trees there was a crack or crevasse in the earth to which he could find no bottom. It was very narrow, but not quite narrow enough to jump. There seemed also to be some vapour rising from it which made the further side indistinct: but the vapour was not so thick nor the chasm so wide but that he could see here a spray of foliage and there a stone with deep moss, and in one place falling water that caught the sunlight. His desire to pass and to go on to the Island was sharp, but not to the degree of pain. Mr. Wisdom's words that the eastern and western things were neither wholly real nor wholly illusion, had spread over his mind a feeling of intent, yet quiet, comfort. Some fear was removed: the suspicion, never before wholly laid at rest, that his wanderings might lead him soon or late into the power of the Landlord, had passed away, and with it the gnawing anxiety lest the Island had never existed. The world seemed full of expectation, even as the misty veil between him and the forest seemed both to cover and discover sublimities that were without terror and beauties without sensuality; and every now and then a strengthening of the south wind would make a moment's clearness and show him, withdrawn in unexpected depth, remote reaches of the mountain valleys, desolate fields of flowers, the hint of snow beyond. He lay down in the grass. Presently one of the young men of the house passed that way and stopped to talk with him. They spoke of this and that, lazily, and at long intervals. Sometimes they discussed the regions further South where John had not been; sometimes, his own travels. The young man told him that if he had followed the road a few miles beyond the valley he would have come to a fork. The left hand turn would lead you, by a long way round, to the parts about Claptrap: the right went on to the southern forests, to the city of the Magicians and the country of Nycteris, 'and beyond that it is all swamp and sugar cane,' said he, 'and crocodiles and venomous spiders until the land sinks away altogether into the final salt swamp which becomes at last the southern ocean. There are no settlements there except a few lakedwellers, Theosophists and what not, and it is very malarial.'

While they were speaking of the parts that John already knew, he asked his informant whether they in the House of Wisdom knew anything of the Grand Canyon or of the way down into it.

'Do you not know?' said the other, 'that we are in the bottom of the canyon here?' Then he made John sit up and showed him the lie of the land. The sides of the valley drew together northward, and at the same time grew more precipitous, so that at last they came together into a great V. 'And that V is the canyon, and you are looking into it endways from the southern end. The eastern face of the canyon is gentle and you were walking down into it all day yesterday, though you did not notice it.'

'So I am in the bottom of it already,' said John. 'And now there is nothing to prevent me from crossing it.'

The young man shook his head.

'There is no crossing it,' he said. 'When I told you we were now at the bottom, I meant the lowest point that can be reached by man. The real bottom is, of course, the bottom of this crevasse which we are sitting by: and that, of course—well, it would be a misunderstanding to talk of getting down it. There is no question of crossing or of getting to what you see over there.'

'Could it not be bridged?' said John.

'In a sense there is nothing to bridge—there is nowhere for this bridge to *arrive at*. You must not take literally the show of forest and mountain which we seem to see as we look across.'

'You don't mean that it is an illusion?'

'No. You will understand better when you have been longer with my father. It is not an illusion, it is an appearance. It is a true appearance, too, in a sense. You *must* see it as a mountain-side or the like—a continuation of the world we *do* know—and it does not mean that there is anything wrong with your eyes or any better way of seeing it to which you can attain. But don't think you can get there. Don't think there is any meaning in the idea of you (a man) going "there", as if it were really a place.'

'What? And the Island too! You would have me give up my heart's desire?'

'I would not. I would not have you cease to fix all your desires on the far side, for to wish to cross is simply to be a man, and to lose that wish is to be a beast. It is not desire that my father's doctrine kills: it is only hope.'

'And what is this valley called?'

'We call it now simply Wisdom's Valley: but the oldest maps mark it as the Valley of Humiliation.'

'The grass is quite wet,' said John, after a pause. 'The dew is beginning.'

'It is time that we went to supper,' said the young man.

CHAPTER NINE

Wisdom—Exoteric

NEXT day, as before, Wisdom had John and Vertue into the porch and continued to instruct them;

'You have heard what you are not to think of the eastern and western things, and now let us discover, as far as the imperfection of our faculty allows, what may rightly be thought. And first, consider this country in which we live. You see that it is full of roads, and no man remembers the making of these roads: neither have we any way to describe and order the land in our minds except by reference to them. You have seen how we determine the position of every other place by its relation to the main road: and though you may say that we have maps, you are to consider that the maps would be useless without the roads, for we find where we are on the map by the skeleton of roads which is common to it and to the country. We see that we have just passed such a turn to the right or the left, or that we are approaching such a bend in the road, and thus we know that we are near to some other place on the map which is not yet visible on the countryside. The people, indeed, say that the Landlord made these roads: and the Claptrapians say that we first made them on the map and have projected them, by some strange process, from it to the country. But I would have you hold fast to the truth, that we find them and do not make them: but also that no *man* could make them. For to make them he would need a bird's-eye view of the whole country, which he could have only from the sky. But no man could live in the sky. Again, this country is full of rules. The Claptrapians say that the Stewards made the rules. The servants of the giant say that we made them ourselves in order to restrain by them the lusts of our neighbours and to give a pompous colouring to our own. The people say that the Landlord made them.

'Let us consider these doctrines one by one. The Stewards made them? How then came they to be Stewards, and why did the rest of us consent to their rules? As soon as we ask this question, we are obliged to ask another. How comes it that those who have rejected the Stewards immediately set about making new rules of their own, and that these new rules are substantially the same as the old? A man says, 'I have finished with rules: henceforth I will do what I want:" but he finds that his deepest want, the only want that is constant through the flux of his appetites and despondencies, his moments of calm and of passion, is to keep the rules. Because these rules are a disguise for his desires, say the giant's following. But, I ask, what desires? Not any and every desire: the rules are frequently denials of these desires. The desire for self-approbation, shall we say? But why should we approve ourselves for keeping the rules unless we already thought that the rules were good? A man may find pleasure in supposing himself swifter or stronger than he really is, but only if he already loves speed or strength. The giant's doctrine thus destroys itself. If we wish to give a seemly colouring to our lusts we have already the idea of the seemly, and the seemly turns out to be nothing else than that which is according to the rules. The want to obey the rules is this presupposed in every doctrine which describes our obedience to them, or the rules themselves, as a self-flattery. Let us turn then to the old tale of the Landlord. Some mighty man beyond this country has made the rules. Suppose he has: then why do we obey them?'

Mr. Wisdom turned to Vertue and said, 'This part is of great concern to you and to your cure,' then he continued:

'There can be only two reasons. Either because we respect the power of the Landlord, and are moved by fear of the penalties and hopes of the rewards with which he sanctions the rules: or else, because we freely agree with the Landlord, because we also think good the things that he thinks good. But neither explanation will serve. If we obey through hope and fear, in that very act we disobey: for the rule which we reverence most, whether we find it in our own hearts or on the Steward's card, is that rule which says that a man must act disinterestedly. To obey the Landlord thus, would be to disobey. But what if we obey freely, because we agree with him? Alas, this is even worse. To say that we agree, and obey because we agree, is only to say again that we find the same rule written in our hearts and obey *that*. If the Landlord enjoins *that*, he enjoins only what we already purposed to do, and

127

his voice is idle: if he enjoins anything else, his voice is again is idle, for we shall disobey him. In either case the mystery of the rules remains unsolved, and the Landlord is a meaningless addition to the problem. If he spoke, the rules were there before he spoke. If we and he agree about them, where is the common original which he and we both copy: what is the thing about which his doctrine and ours are both true?

'Of the rules, then as of the roads, we must say that indeed we find them and do not make them, but that it helps us not at all to assume a Landlord for their maker. And there is a third thing also' (here he looked to John) 'which specially concerns you. What of the Island in the West? The People in our age have all but forgotten it. The giant would say that it is, again, a delusion in your own mind trumped up to conceal lust. Of the Stewards, some do not know that there is such a thing: some agree with the giant, denouncing your Island as wicked-ness: some say that it is a blurred and confused sight from far off of the Landlord's castle. They have no common doctrine: but let us consider the question for ourselves.

'And first I would have you set aside all suspicion that the giant is right: and this will be the easier for you because you have already talked with Reason. They say it is there to conceal lust. But it does not conceal lust. If it is a screen, it is a very bad screen. The giant would make the dark part of our mind so strong and subtle that we never escape from its deceptions: and yet when this omnipotent conjuror has done all that he can, he produces an illusion which a solitary boy, in the fancies of his adolescence, can expose and see through in two years. This is but wild talk. There is no man and no nation at all capable of seeing the Island, who have not learned by experience, and that soon, how easily the vision ends in lust: and there is none also, not corrupted, who has not felt the disappointment of that ending, who has not known that it is the breaking of the vision not its consummation. The words between you and Reason were true. What does not satisfy when we find it, was not the thing we were desiring. If water will not set a man at ease, then be sure it was not thirst, or not thirst only, that tormented him: he wanted drunkenness to cure his dullness, or talk to cure his solitude, or the like. How, indeed, do we know our desires save by their satisfaction?

When do we know them until we say, "Ah, *this* was what I wanted"?
And if there were any desire which it was natural for man to feel but
impossible for man to satisfy, would not the nature of this desire remain
to him always ambiguous? If old tales were true, if a man without
putting off humanity could indeed pass the frontiers of our country, if
he could be, and yet be a man, in that fabled East and fabled West,
then indeed at the moment of fruition, the raising of the cup, the
assumption of the crown, the kiss of the spouse—then first, to his
backward glance, the long roads of desire that he had trodden would
become plain in all their winding, and when he found, he would know
what it was that he had sought. I am old and full of tears, and I see that
you also begin to feel the sorrow that is born with us. Abandon hope:
do not abandon desire. Feel no wonder that these glimpses of your
Island so easily confuse themselves with viler things, and are so easily
blasphemed. Above all, never try to keep them, never try to revisit the
same place or time wherein the vision was accorded to you. You will
pay the penalty of all who would bind down to one place or time
within our country that which our country cannot contain. Have you
not heard from the Stewards of the sin of idolatry, and how, in their old
chronicles, the manna turned to worms if any tried to hoard it? Be not
greedy, be not passionate; you will but crush dead on your own breast
with hot, rough hands the thing you loved. But if ever you incline to
doubt that the thing you long for is something real, remember what your
own experience has taught you. Think that it is a *feeling,* and at once
the feeling has no value. Stand sentinel at your own mind, watching
for that feeling, and you will find—what shall I say?—a flutter in the
heart, an image in the head, a sob in the throat: and was *that* your
desire? You know that it was not, and that no feeling whatever will
appease you, that *feeling,* refine it as you will, is but one more spurious
claimant—spurious as the gross lusts of which the giant speaks. Let us
conclude then that what you desire is no state of yourself at all, but
something, for that very reason, Other and Outer. And knowing this
you will find tolerable the truth that you cannot attain it. That the
thing should *be,* is so great a good that when you remember "it is" you
will forget to be sorry that you can never have it. Nay, anything that
you could have would be so much less than this that its fruition would

be immeasurably below the mere hunger for this. Wanting is better than having. The glory of any world wherein you can live is in the end appearance: but then, as one of my sons has said, that leaves the world more glorious yet.'

CHAPTER TEN

Wisdom—Esoteric

THAT day John spent as he had spent the other, wandering and often sleeping in the fields. In this valley the year came on with seven-leagued boots. To-day the riverside was thick with fritillaries, the kingfisher flew, the dragon-flies darted, and when he sat it was in the shade. A pleasing melancholy rested upon him, and a great indolence. He talked that day with many of the people of the house, and when he went that night to his cell his mind was full of their resigned voices, and of their faces, so quiet and yet so alert, as though they waited in hourly expectation of something that would never happen. When next he opened his eyes moonlight filled his cell; and as he lay waking heard a low whistle from without his window. He put out his head. A dark figure stood in the shadow of the house. 'Come out and play,' said he. At the same time there came a sound of suppressed laughter from an angle of deeper shadow beyond the speaker.

'This window is too high for me to jump from,' said John.

'You forget that it is by moonlight,' said the other, and held up his hands.

'Jump!' he said.

John cast some clothes about him and bounded from the window. To his surprise, he reached the ground with no hurt or shock, and a moment later he found himself progressing over the lawn in a series of great leaps amidst a laughing crowd of the sons and daughters of the house: so that the valley in the moonlight, if any had watched, would have looked like nothing so much as a great salver which had been made into the arema for a troupe of performing fleas. Their dance or race, led them to the dark border of a neighbouring wood and as John

130

tumbled down breathless at the foot of a hawthorn, he heard with surprise all around him the sounds of silver and glass, of hampers opening, and bottles uncorking.

'My father's ideas of feeding are a little strict,' explained his host, 'and we younger ones have found it necessary to supplement the household meals a bit.'

'Here is champagne, from Mr. Halfways,' said one.

'Cold chicken and tongue from Mr. Mammon. What *should* we do without our friends?'

'Hashish from the south. Nycteris sent it up herself.'

'This claret,' said a girl beside him rather shyly, 'is from Mother Kirk.'

'I don't think we ought to drink that,' said another voice, 'that is really going a bit too far.'

'No further than your caviare from the Theosophists,' said the first girl, 'and anyway, I need it. It is only this that keeps me alive.'

'Try some of my brandy,' said another voice. 'All made by Savage's dwarfs.'

'I don't know how you can drink that stuff, Karl.[1] Plain, honest food from Claptrap is what you need.'

'So *you* say, Herbert[2],' retorted a new speaker. 'But some of us find it rather heavy. For me, a morsel of lamb from the Shepherd's Country and a little mint sauce—that is really all you need to add to our Father's table.'

'We all know what you like, Benedict,'[3] said several.

'I have finished,' announced Karl, 'and now for a night with the dwarfs. Anyone come with me?'

'Not there,' cried another. 'I'm going South to-night to the magicians.'

'You had much better not, Rudolph[4],' said someone. 'A few quiet hours in Puritania with me would be much better for you—much better.'

'Chuck it, Immanuel[5],' said another. 'You might as well go to Mother Kirk straight away.'

---

[1] Marx   [2] Spencer   [3] Spinoza
[4] Steiner   [5] Kant

'Bernard[1] does,' said the girl, who had contributed the claret.

By this time the party was rapidly decreasing, for most of the young people, after trying in vain to win converts to their several schemes of pleasure, had bounded off alone, plunging from treetop to treetop, and soon even the thin silvery sound of their laughter had died away. Those who were left swarmed round John soliciting his attention now for this, now for that, amusement. Some sat down beyond the shadow of the wood to work out puzzles in the light of the moon: others settled to serious leap-frog: the more frivolous ran to and fro chasing the moths, wrestling with and tickling one another, giggling and making giggle, till the wood rang with their shrill squeals of glee. It seemed to go on for a long time and if there was any more in that dream John did not remember it when he woke.

CHAPTER ELEVEN

Mum's the Word

AT breakfast on the following morning John stole many furtive glances at the sons and daughters of Wisdom, but he could see no sign that they were conscious of having met him in such different guise during the night. Indeed, neither then, nor at any other time during his stay in the valley, did he find evidence that they were aware of their nocturnal holidays: and a few tentative questions assured him that, unless they were liars, they all believed themselves to be living exclu- sively on the spare diet of the house. Immanuel indeed admitted, as a speculative truth, that there were such things as dreams, and that he conceivably dreamed himself: but then he had a complex proof (which John never quite grasped) that no one could possibly remember a dream: and though his appearance and constitution were those of a prize-fighter he attributed this all to the excellent quality of the local fruit. Herbert was a lumpish sort of man who never could muster any appetite for his meals: but John discovered that Herbert put this down to his liver and had no notion that he had been stuffing himself with

[1] Bosanquet

Claptrapian steak and gravy all night as hard as he could. Another of the family, Bernard by name, was in radiant health. John had seen him drinking Mother Kirk's wine with great relish and refreshment by moon- light: but the waking Bernard maintained that Mother Kirk's wine was merely a bad, early attempt at the admirable barley-water which his father sometimes brought out on birthdays and great occasions; and 'to this barley-water,' he said, 'I owe my health. It has made me what I am.' Still less could John discover, by all the traps that he laid for them, whether the younger members of the household had any recollection of their nightly leap-frog and other gambols. He was forced at last to conclude that either the whole thing had been a private dream of his own or else the secret was very well kept. A little irritation which some displayed when he questioned them, seemed to favour the second hypothesis.

CHAPTER TWELVE

More Wisdom

WHEN they were seated in the porch, Wisdom continued his discourse.

'You have learned that there are these three things, the Island, the Roads, and the Rules: that they are certainly in some way real and that we have not made them; and further that it does not help us to invent a Landlord. Nor is it possible that there should really be a castle at one end of the world and an island at the other: for the world is round and we are everywhere at the end of the world, since the end of a sphere is its surface. The world is *all* end: but we can never pass beyond that end. And yet these things which our imagination impossibly places as a world beyond the world's end are, we have seen, in some sense real.

'You have told me how Reason refuted the lies of the giant by asking what was the colour of things in dark places. You learned from her that there is no colour without seeing, no hardness without touching: no *body*, to say all, save in the minds of those who perceive it. It follows, then, that all this choir of heaven and furniture of earth are imagina- tions: not your imaginations nor mine, for here we have met in the

133

same world, which could not be if the world was shut up within my mind or yours. Without doubt, then, all this show of sky and earth floats within some mighty imagination. If you ask Whose, again the Landlord will not help you. He is a man: make him as great as you will, he still is other than we and his imagining inaccessible to us, as yours would be to me. Rather we must say that the world is not in this mind, or in that, but in Mind itself, in that impersonal principle of consciousness which flows eternally through us, its perishable forms.

'You see how this explains all the questions that have lain on our knees since we began. We find the roads, the reasonable skeleton in the countryside, the guiding-lines that enable us both to make maps and to use them when we have made, because our country is the off-spring of the rational. Consider also the Island. All that you know of it comes at last to this: that your first sight of it was yearning or wanting and that you have never ceased to want that first sight back, as though you wanted a wanting, as though the wanting were the having, and the having a wanting. What is the meaning of this hungry fruition and this emptiness which is the best filling? Surely, it becomes plain when you have learned that no man says "I" in an unambiguous sense. I am an old man who must soon go over the brook and be seen no more: I am eternal Mind in which time and place themselves are contained. I am the Imaginer: I am one of his imaginations. The Island is nothing else than that perfection and immortality which I possess as Spirit eternal, and vainly crave as mortal soul. Its voices sound at my very ear and are further than the stars; it is under my hand and will never be mine: I have it and lo! the very having is the losing: because at every moment I, as Spirit, am indeed abandoning my rich estate to become that perishing and imperfect creature in whose repeated deaths and births stands my eternity. And I as man in every moment still enjoy the perfection I have lost, since still, so far as I am at all, I am Spirit, and only by being Spirit maintain my short vitality as soul. See how life subsists by death and each becomes the other: for Spirit lives by dying perpetually into such things as we, and we also attain our truest life by dying to our mortal nature and relapsing, as far as may be, into the impersonality of our source: for this is the final meaning of all moral precepts, and the goodness of temperance and justice and of love itself is that they plunge the red heat of our separate and individual passions back in the ice brook of the Spirit, there to take eternal temper, though not endless duration.

'What I tell you is the *evangelium eternum*. This has been known always: ancients and moderns bear witness to it. The stories of the Landlord in our own time are but a picture-writing which show to the people as much of the truth as they can understand. Stewards must have told you—though it seems that you neither heeded nor understood them—the legend of the Landlord's Son. They say that after the eating of the mountain-apple and the earthquake, when things in our country had gone all awry, the Landlord's Son himself became one of his Father's tenants and lived among us, for no other purpose than that he should be killed. The Stewards themselves do not know clearly the meaning of their story: hence, if you ask them how the slaying of the Son should help us. they are driven to monstrous answers. But to us the meaning is clear and the story is beautiful. It is a picture of the life of Spirit itself. What the Son is in the legend, every man is in reality: for the whole world is nothing else than the Eternal thus giving itself to death that it may live—that we may live. Death is life's mode, and the increase of life is through repeated death.

'And what of the rules? You have seen that it is idle to make them the arbitrary commands of a Landlord: yet those who do so were not altogether astray, for it is equally an error to think that they are each man's personal choice. Remember what we have said of the Island. Because I am and am not Spirit, therefore I have and have not my desire. The same double nature of the word "I", explains the rules. I am the lawgiver: but I am also the subject. I, the Spirit, impose upon the soul which I become, the laws she must henceforth obey: and every conflict between the rules and our inclinations is but a conflict of the wishes of my mortal and apparent self against those of my real and eternal. "I ought but I do not wish"—how meaningless the words are, how close to saying, "I want and I do not want." But once we have learned to say "I, and yet not I, want", the mystery is plain.

'And now your sick friend is almost whole, and it is nearly noon.'

135

BOOK EIGHT

AT BAY

He that hath understanding in himself is best;
He that lays up his brother's wisdom in his breast
Is good. But he that neither knoweth, nor will be taught
By the instruction of the wise—this man is naught.—HESIOD

Persons without education certainly do not want either acuteness or strength of mind in what concerns themselves, or in things immediately within their observation; but they have no power of abstraction—they see their objects always near, never in the horizon.
—HAZLITT

CHAPTER ONE

Two Kinds of Monist

THAT afternoon as John was walking in the water meadow he saw a man coming towards him who walked blunderingly like one whose legs were not his own. And as the man came nearer he saw that it was Vertue, with his face very pale.

'What,' cried John, 'are you cured? Can you see? Can you speak?'

'Yes,' said Vertue in a weak voice, 'I suppose I can see.' And he leaned heavily on a stile and breathed hard.

'You have walked too far,' said John. 'Are you ill?'

'I am still weak. It is nothing. I shall get my breath in a moment.'

'Sit down by me,' said John. 'And when you have rested we will go gently back to the house.'

'I am not going back to the house.'

'Not going back? You are not fit to travel—and where are you going?'

'I am not fit for anything, apparently,' said Vertue. 'But I must go on.'

'Go on where? You are not still hoping to cross the canyon? Do you not believe what Wisdom has told us?'

'I do. That is why I am going on.'

'Sit down at least for a moment,' said John, 'and explain yourself.'

'It is plain enough!'

'It isn't plain at all.'

Vertue spoke impatiently.

'Did you not hear what Wisdom said about the rules?' he asked.

'Of course I did,' said John.

'Well, then, he has given me back the rules. *That* puzzle is solved. The rules have to be obeyed, as I always thought. I know that now better than I have ever known it before.'

'Well?'

'And didn't you see what all the rest came to? The rules are from this Spirit or whatever he calls it, which is somehow also me. And any

138

disinclination to obey the rules is the other part of me—the mortal part. Does it not follow from that, and from everything else he said, that the real disobedience to the rules begins with being in this country at all? This country is simply *not* the Island, *not* the rules: that is its definition. My mortal self—that is, for all practical purposes, myself—can be defined only as the part of me that is against the rules. Just as the Spirit answers to the Landlord, so this whole world answers to the black hole.'

'I take it all exactly the other way,' said John. 'Rather this world corresponds to the Landlord's castle. Everything is this Spirit's imagination, and therefore everything, properly understood, is good and happy. That the glory of this world in the end is appearance, leaves the world more glorious yet. I quite agree that the rules—the authority of the rules—becomes stronger than ever: but their content must be—well, easier. Perhaps I should say richer—more concrete.'

'Their content must become harsher. If the real good is simply "what is not here" and *here* means simply "the place where the good is not", what can the real rule be except to live here as little as possible, to commit ourselves as little as we can to the system of this world? I used to talk of innocent pleasures, fool that I was—as if anything could be innocent for us whose mere existence is a fall—as if all that a man eats or drinks or begets were not propagated curse.'

'Really, Vertue, this is a very strange view. The effect of Mr. Wisdom's lessons on me has been just the opposite. I have been thinking how much of the Puritanian virus there must still be in me, to have held me back so long from the blameless generosity of Nature's breasts. Is not the meanest thing, in its degree, a mirror of the One; the lightest or the wildest pleasure as necessary to the perfection of the whole as the most heroic sacrifice? I am assured that in the Absolute, every flame even of carnal passion burns on——'

'Can even eating, even the coarsest food and the barest pittance, be justified? The flesh is but a living corruption——'

'There was a great deal to be said for Media after all——'

'I see that Savage was wiser than he knew——'

'It is true she had a dark complexion. And yet—is not brown as necessary to the spectrum as any other colour?'

'Is not every colour equally a corruption of the white radiance?'

'What we call evil—our greatest wickednesses—seen in the true setting is an element in the good. I am the doubter and the doubt.'

'What we call our righteousness is filthy rags. You are a fool, John, and I am going. I am going up into the rocks till I find where the wind is coldest and the ground hardest and the life of man furthest away. My notice to quit has not yet come, and I must be stained a while longer with the dye of our country. I shall still be part of that dark cloud which offends the white light: but I shall make that part of the cloud which is called Me as thin, as nearly not a cloud, as I can. Body and mind shall pay for the crime of their existence. If there is any fasting, or watching, any mutilation or self-torture more harsh to nature than another, I shall find it out.'

'Are you mad?' said John.

'I have just become sane,' said Vertue, 'Why are you staring at me thus? I know I am pale and my pulse beats like a hammer. So much the saner! Disease is better than health and sees clearer, for it is one degree nearer to the Spirit, one degree less involved in the riot of our animal existence. But it will need stronger pains than this to kill the obscene thirst for life which I drank in with my mother's milk.'

'Why should we leave this pleasant valley?' John began, but Vertue cut him short.

'Who spoke of We? Do you think that I asked or expected *you* to accompany me? *You* to sleep on thorns and eat sloes?'

'You don't mean that we are to part?' said John.

'Pah!' said Vertue. 'You could not do the things I intend to do: and if you could, I would have none of you. Friendship—affection—what are these but the subtlest chains that tie us to our present country? He would be a fool indeed who mortified the body and left the mind free to be happy and thus still to affirm—to wallow in—her finite will. It is not this pleasure or that, but *all* that are to be cut off. No knife will cut deep enough to end the cancer. But I'll cut as deep as I can.'

He rose, still swaying, and continued his way over the meadow northward. He held his hand to his side as though he was in pain. Once or twice he nearly fell.

'What are you following me for?' he shouted to John. 'Go back.'

John stopped for a moment, checked by the hatred in his friend's face. Then, tentatively, he went on again. He thought that Vertue's illness had harmed his brain and had some indistinct hope that he might find means to humour him and bring him back. Before they had gone many paces, however, Vertue turned again and lifted a stone in his hand. 'Be off,' he said, 'or I'll throw it. We have nothing to do with one another, you and I. My own body and my own soul are enemies, and do you think I will spare *you*?'

John halted, undetermined, and then ducked, for the other had hurled the stone. I saw them go on like this for some way, John following at a distance, and stopping, and then continuing again, while Vertue every now and then stoned him and reviled him. But at last the distance between them was too great either for voice or stone to carry.

CHAPTER TWO

John Led

As they went on thus John saw that the valley narrowed and the sides of it grew steeper. At the same time, the crevasse on his left hand which separated him from the western forest, became wider and wider: so that, what with that, and with the narrowing of the valley as a whole, the level piece where they were travelling was constantly diminished. Soon it was no longer the floor of the valley but only a ledge on its eastern side: and the crevasse revealed itself as being not a slot in the floor but the very floor. John saw that he was, in fact, walking on a shelf half-way down one side of the Grand Canyon. The cliff towered above him.

Presently a kind of spur or root of rock came out from the cliff and barred their way—crossing the ledge with a ruin of granite. And as Vertue began to scramble about the bases of this ascent, trying this grip and that to go up, John gained on him and came again within earshot. Before he came to the foot of the crags, however, Vertue had begun to climb. John heard his gasping as he struggled from hold to hold. Once he slipped back and left a little trail of blood where the rock skinned his ankle: but he went on again, and soon John saw him stand up, shaking and wiping the sweat out of his eyes, apparently at the top. He looked down and made gestures threateningly, and shouted, but he was too far for John to hear his words. Next moment John leaped aside to save his limbs, for Vertue had sent a great boulder rolling down: and as its thunder ceased echoing in the gorge and John looked up again, Vertue had gone over the spur out of sight and he saw no more of him.

John sat down in the desolate place. The grass here was finer and shorter, such grass as sheep love, which grows in the quiet intervals between the rocks. The windings of the gorge had already shut off the sight of Wisdom's Valley: yet I saw that John had no thought save of going back. There was indeed a confusion of shame and sorrow and bewilderment in his mind, but he put it all aside and held fast to his fear of the rocks and of meeting Vertue, now mad, in some narrow place whence he could not retreat. He thought, 'I will sit here and rest, till I get my wind, and then I will go back. I must live out the rest of my life as best I can.' Then suddenly he heard himself hailed from above. A Man was descending where Vertue had gone up.

'Hi!' shouted the Man. 'Your friend has gone on. Surely you will follow him?'

'He is mad, sir,' said John.

'No madder than you, and no saner,' said the Man. 'You will both recover if only you will keep together.'

'I cannot get up the rocks,' said John.

'I will give you a hand,' said the Man. And he came down till he was within reach of John, and held out his hand. And John grew pale as paper and nausea came upon him.

'It's now or never,' said the Man.

Then John set his teeth and took the hand that was offered him. He trembled at the very first grip he was made to take but he could not go back for they were speedily so high that he dared not attempt the return alone: and what with pushing and pulling the Man got him right up to the top and there he fell down on his belly in the grass to pant and to groan at the pains in his chest. When he sat up the Man was gone.

CHAPTER THREE

John Forgets Himself

JOHN looked back and turned away with a shudder. All thought of descending again must be put aside at once and for ever. 'That fellow has left me in a nice fix,' he said bitterly. Next, he looked ahead. The cliffs still rose high above him and dropped far below him: but there was a ledge on a level with him, a narrow ledge, ten feet broad at its best and two at its worst, winding away along the cliff till it became but a green thread. His heart failed him. Then he tried to recall the lessons of Mr. Wisdom, whether they would give him any strength. 'It is only myself,' he said. 'It is I myself, eternal Spirit, who drive this Me, the slave, along that ledge. I ought not to care whether he falls and breaks his neck or not. It is not he that is real, it is I—I—I. Can I remember that?' But then he felt so different from the eternal Spirit that he could call it 'I' no longer. 'It is all very well for *him*,' said John, 'but why does he give me no help? I want help. Help.' Then he gazed up at the cliffs and the narrow sky, blue and remote, between them, and he thought of that universal mind and of the shining tranquillity hidden somewhere behind the colours and the shapes, the pregnant silence under all the sounds, and he thought, 'If one drop of all that ocean would flow into me now—if I, the mortal, could but realize that I *am* that, all would be well. I know there is something there. I know the sensuous curtain is not a cheat,' In the bitterness of his soul he looked up again, saying: 'Help. Help. I want Help.'

But as soon as the words were out of his mouth, a new fear, far deeper than his fear of the cliffs, sprang at him from the hiding-place, close to the surface, where it had lain against this moment. As a man in a dream talks without fear to his dead friend, and only afterwards bethinks himself, 'It was a ghost! I have talked with a ghost!' and wakes screaming: even so John sprang up as he saw what he had done.

'I have been *praying*,' he said. 'It is the Landlord under a new name. It is the rules and the black hole and the slavery dressed out in a new

143

fashion to catch me. And I am caught. Who would have thought the old spider's web was so subtle?'

But this was insupportable to him and he said that he had only fallen into a metaphor. Even Mr. Wisdom had confessed that Mother Kirk and the Stewards gave an account of the truth in picture writing. And one must use metaphors. The feelings and the imagination needed that support. 'The great thing,' said John, 'is to keep the intellect free from them: to remember that they *are* metaphors.'

CHAPTER FOUR

John Finds his Voice

HE was much comforted by this idea of metaphor, and as he was now also rested, he began his journey along the cliff path with some degree of timid resolution. But it was very dreadful to him in the narrower places: and his courage seemed to him to decrease rather than to grow as he proceeded. Indeed he soon found that he could go forward at all only by remembering Mr. Wisdom's Absolute incessantly. It was necessary by repeated efforts of the will to turn thither, consciously to draw from that endless reservoir the little share of vitality that he needed for the next narrow place. He knew now that he was praying, but he thought that he had drawn the fangs of that knowledge. In a sense, he said, Spirit is not I. I am it, but I am not the whole of it. When I turn back to that part of it which is not I—that far greater part which my soul does not exhaust—surely that part is to me an Other. It must become, for my imagination, not really 'I' but 'Thou'. A metaphor—perhaps more than a metaphor. Of course there is no need at all to confuse it with the *mythical* Landlord. . . . However I think of it, I think of it inadequately.

Then a new thing happened to John, and he began to sing: and this is as much of his song as I remember from my dream

> He whom I bow to only knows to whom I bow
> When I attempt the ineffable name, murmuring *Thou*;

And dream of Pheidian fancies and embrace in heart
Meanings, I know, that cannot be the thing thou art.
All prayers always, taken at their word, blaspheme,
Invoking with frail imageries a folk-lore dream;
And all men are idolaters, crying unheard
To senseless idols, if thou take them at their word,
And all men in their praying, self-deceived, address
One that is not (so saith that old rebuke) unless
Thou, of mere grace, appropriate, and to thee divert
Men's arrows, all at hazard aimed, beyond desert.
Take not, oh Lord, our literal sense, but in thy great,
Unbroken speech our halting metaphor translate.

When he came to think over the words that had gone out of him he began once more to be afraid of them. Day was declining and in the narrow chasm it was already almost dark.

CHAPTER FIVE

Food at a Cost

FOR a while he went on cautiously, but he was haunted by a picture in his mind of a place where the path would break off short when it was too dark for him to see, and he would step on air. This fear made him halt more and more frequently to examine his ground: and when he went on it was each time more slowly: till at last he came to a stand-still. There seemed to be nothing for it but to rest where he was. The night was warm, but he was both hungry and thirsty. And he sat down. It was quite dark now.

Then I dreamed that once more a Man came to him in the darkness and said, 'You must pass the night where you are, but I have brought you a loaf and if you crawl along the ledge ten paces more you will find that a little fall of water comes down the cliff.'

'Sir,' said John. 'I do not know your name and I cannot see your face, but I thank you. Will you not sit down and eat, yourself?'

145

'I am full and not hungry,' said the Man. 'And I will pass on. But one word before I go. You cannot have it both ways.'

'What do you mean, sir?'

'Your life has been saved all this day by crying out to something which you call by many names, and you have said to yourself that you used metaphors.'

'Was I wrong, sir?'

'Perhaps not. But you must play fair. If its help is not a metaphor, neither are its commands. If it can answer when you call, then it can speak without your asking. If you can go to it, it can come to you.'

'I think I see, sir. You mean that I am not my own man: in some sense I have a Landlord after all?'

'Even so. But what is it that dismays you? You heard from Wisdom how the rules were yours and not yours. Did you not mean to keep them? And if so, can it scare you to know that there is one who will make you able to keep them?'

'Well, said John, 'I suppose you have found me out. Perhaps I did not fully mean to keep them—not all—or not all the time. And yet, in a way, I think I did. It is like a thorn in your finger, sir. You know when you set about taking it out yourself—you mean to get it out—you know it will hurt—and it does hurt—but somehow it is not very serious business—well, I suppose, because you feel that you always *could* stop if it was very bad. Not that you intend to stop. But it is a very different thing to hold your hand out to a surgeon to be hurt as much as *he* thinks fit. And at *his* speed.'

The Man laughed, 'I see you understand me very well,' He said, 'but the great thing is to get the thorn out.' And then He went away.

CHAPTER SIX

Caught

JOHN had no difficulty in finding the stream and when he had drunk he sat by it and ate. The bread had a rather flat taste which was somehow familiar and not very agreeable, but he was in no position to be dainty. Extreme weariness prevented him from thinking much of the conversation that had just passed. At the bottom of John's heart the stranger's words lay like a cold weight that he must some day take up and carry: but his mind was full of the pictures of cliff and chasm, of wondering about Vertue, and of smaller fears for the morrow and the moment, and, above all, the blessedness of food and of sitting still; and all these jumbled themselves together in an even dimmer confusion till at last he could no longer remember which he had been thinking of the moment before: and then he knew that he was sleeping: and at last he was in deep sleep and knew nothing.

In the morning it was not so. Jump with his first waking thought the full-grown horror leaped upon him. The blue sky above the cliffs was watching him: the cliffs themselves were imprisoning him: the rocks behind were cutting off his retreat: the path ahead was ordering him on. In one night the Landlord—call him by what name you would—had come back to the world, and filled the world, quite full without a cranny. His eyes stared and His hand pointed and His voice commanded in everything that could be heard or seen, even from this place where John sat, to the end of the world: and if you passed the end of the world He would be there too. All things were indeed one— more truly one than Mr. Wisdom dreamed—and all things said one word: CAUGHT—Caught into slavery again, to walk warily and on sufferance all his days, never to be alone; never the master of his own soul, to have no privacy, no corner whereof you could say to the whole universe: This is my own, here I can do as I please. Under that universal and inspecting gaze, John cowered like some small animal caught up in a giant's hands and held beneath a magnifying-glass.

When he had drunk and splashed his face in the stream he continued his way, and presently he made this song.

> You rest upon me all my days
> The inevitable Eye,
> Dreadful and undeflected as the blaze
> Of some Arabian sky;
>
> Where, dead still, in their smothering tent
> Pale travellers crouch, and, bright

About them, noon's long-drawn Astonishment
Hammers the rocks with light.

Oh, for but one cool breath in seven,
One air from northern climes,
The changing and the castle-clouded heaven
Of my old Pagan times!

But you have seized all in your rage
Of Oneness. Round about,
Beating my wings, all ways, within your cage,
I flutter, but not out.

And as he walked on, all day, in the strength of the bread he had eaten, not daring often to look down into the gulf and keeping his head mostly turned a little inward to the cliff, he had time to turn his trouble over in his mind and discover new sides to it. Above all it grew upon him that the return of the Landlord had blotted out the Island: for if there still were such a place he was no longer free to spend his soul in seeking it, but must follow whatever designs the Landlord had for him. And at the very best it now seemed that the last of things was at least more like a person than a place, so that the deepest thirst within him was not adapted to the deepest nature of the world. But sometimes he comforted himself by saying that this new and real Land-lord must yet be very different from him whom the Stewards proclaimed and indeed from all images that men could make of him. There might still hang about him some of that promising darkness which had covered the Absolute.

CHAPTER SEVEN

The Hermit

PRESENTLY he heard a bell struck, and he looked and saw a little chapel in a cave of the cliff beside him; and there sat a hermit whose name was History, so old and thin that his hands were transparent and John thought that a little wind would have blown him away.

148

'Turn in, my son,' said the hermit, 'and eat bread and then you shall go on your journey.' John was glad to hear the voice of a man among the rocks and he turned in and sat. The hermit gave him bread and water but he himself ate no bread and drank a little wine.

'Where are you going, son?' he said.

'It seems to me, Father, that I am going where I do not wish; for I set out to find an Island and I have found a Landlord instead.'

And the hermit sat looking at him, nodding almost imperceptibly with the tremors of age.

'The Clevers were right and the pale men were right,' said John, thinking aloud, 'since the world holds no allaying for the thirst I was born with, and seemingly the Island was an illusion after all. But I forget, Father, that you will not know these people.'

'I know all parts of this country,' said the hermit, 'and the genius of places. Where do these people live?'

'To the North of the road. The Clevers are in the country of Mammon, where a stone giant is the lord of the soil, and the pale men are on the Tableland of the Tough-Minded.'

'I have been in these countries a thousand times, for in my young days I was a pedlar and there is no land I have not been in. But tell me, do they still keep their old customs?'

'What customs were those?'

'Why, they all sprang from the ownership of the land there, for more than half of the country North of the road is now held by the Enemy's tenants. Eastward it was the giant, and under him Mammon and some others. But westward, on the Tableland, it was two daughters of the Enemy—let me see—yes, Ignorantia and Superbia. They always did impose strange customs on the smaller tenants. I remember many tenants there—Stoics and Manichees, Spartiates, and all sorts. One time they had a notion to eat better bread than is made of wheat. Another time their very nurses took up a strange ritual of always emptying the baby out along with the bath. Then once the Enemy sent a fox without a tail among them and it persuaded them that all animals should be without tails and they docked all their dogs and horses and cows. I remember they were very puzzled how to apply any corresponding treatment to themselves, until at last a wise man suggested that they could cut off their noses. But the strangest custom of all was one that they practised all the time through all their other changes of customs. It was this—that they never set anything to rights but destroyed it instead.' When a dish was dirty they did not wash it, they broke it; and when their clothes were dirty they burned them.'

'It must have been a very expensive custom.'

'It was ruinous, and it meant, of course, that they were constantly importing new clothes and new crockery. But indeed they had to import everything for that is the difficulty of the Tableland. It never has been able to support life and it never will. Its inhabitants have always lived on their neighbours.'

'They must always have been very rich men.'

'They always *were* very rich men. I don't think I remember a single case of a poor or a common person going there. When humble people go wrong they generally go South. The Tough-Minded nearly always go to the Tableland as colonists from Mammon's country. I would guess that your pale men are reformed Clevers.'

'In a kind of way I believe they are. But can you tell me, Father, why these Tough-Minded people behave so oddly?'

'Well, for one thing, they *know* very little. They never travel and consequently never learn anything. They really do not know that there are any places outside Mammon's country and their own Tableland—except that they have heard exaggerated rumours about the Southern swamps, and suppose that everything is swamp a few miles South or themselves. Thus, their disgust with bread came about through sheer ignorance. At home in Mammon's country they knew only the standard bread that Mammon makes, and a few sweet, sticky cakes which Mammon imported from the South—the only kind of Southern product that Mammon would be likely to let in. As they did not like either of these, they invented a biscuit of their own. It never occurred to them to walk a mile off the Tableland into the nearest cottage and try what an honest loaf tasted like. The same with the babies. They disliked babies because babies meant to them the various deformities spawned in the brothels of Mammon: again, a moderate walk would have shown them healthy children at play in the lanes. As for their poor noses—on the Tableland there is nothing to smell, good, bad, or indifferent, and in Mammon's land whatever does not reek of scent reeks of ordure. So they saw no good in noses, though five miles away from them the hay was being cut.'

'And what about the Island, Father?' said John. 'Were they equally wrong about that?'

'That is a longer story, my son. But I see it is beginning to rain, so perhaps you may as well hear it.'

John went to the mouth of the cave and looked out. The sky had grown dark while they talked and a warm rain, blotting out the cliffs like a steam, was descending as far as his eye could reach.

CHAPTER EIGHT

History's Words

WHEN John had returned and seated himself, the hermit resumed:

'You may be sure that they make the same mistake about the Island that they make about everything else. But what is the current lie at present?'

'They say it is all a device of Mr. Halfways—who is in the pay of the Brown Girls.'

'Poor Halfways! They treat him very unfairly—as if he were anything more than the local representative of a thing as widespread and as necessary (though, withal, as dangerous) as the sky! Not a bad representative, either, if you take his songs in your stride and use them as they are meant to be used: of course people who go to him in cold blood to get as much *pleasure* as they can, and therefore hear the same song over and over again, have only themselves to thank if they wake in the arms of Media.'

'That is very true, Father. But they wouldn't believe that I had seen and longed for the Island before I met Mr. Halfways—before I ever heard a song at all. They insist on treating it as his invention.'

'That is always the way with stay-at-homes. If they like somthing in their own village they take it for a thing universal and eternal, though perhaps it was never heard of five miles away; if they dislike something, they say it is a local, backward, provincial convention, though, in fact, it may be the law of nations.'

'Then it is really true that all men, all nations, have had this vision of an Island?'

'It does not always come in the form of an Island: and to some men, if they inherit particular diseases, it may not come at all.'

'But what *is* it, Father? And has it anything to do with the Landlord? I do not know how to fit things together.'

'It comes from the Landlord. We know this by its results. It has brought you to where you now are: and nothing leads back to him which did not at first proceed from him.'

'But the Stewards would say that it was the Rules which come from him.'

'Not all Stewards are equally travelled men. But those who are, know perfectly well that the Landlord has circulated other things besides the Rules. What use are Rules to people who cannot read?'

'But nearly everyone can.'

'No one is born able to read: so that the starting point for all of us must be a picture and not the Rules. And there are more than you suppose who are illiterate all their lives, or who, at the best, never learn to read well.'

'And for these people the pictures are the right thing?'

'I would not quite say that. The pictures alone are dangerous, and the Rules alone are dangerous. That is why the best thing of all is to find Mother Kirk at the very beginning, and to live from infancy with a third thing which is neither the Rules nor the pictures and which was brought into the country by the Landlord's Son. That, I say, is the best: never to have known the quarrel between the Rules and the pictures. But it very rarely happens. The Enemy's agents are everywhere at work, spreading illiteracy in one district and blinding men to the pictures in another. Even where Mother Kirk is nominally the ruler men can grow old without knowing how to read the Rules. Her empire is always crumbling. But it never quite crumbles: for as often as men become Pagans again, the Landlord again sends them pictures and stirs up sweet desire and so leads them back to Mother Kirk even as he led the actual Pagans long ago. There is, indeed, no other way.'

'Pagans?' said John. 'I do not know that people.'

'I forgot that you had travelled so little. It may well be that you were never in the country of Pagus in the flesh, though in another sense, you have lived there all your life. The curious thing about Pagus was that the people there had not heard of the Landlord.'

'Surely, a great many other people don't know either?'

'Oh, a great many *deny* his existence. But you have to be told about a thing before you can deny it. The pecularity of the Pagans was that they had not been told: or if they had, it is so long ago that the tradition had died out. You see, the Enemy had practically supplanted the Landlord, and he kept a sharp watch against any news from that quarter reaching the tenants.'

'Did he succeed?'

'No. It is commonly thought that he did, but that is a mistake. It is commonly thought that he fuddled the tenants by circulating a mass of false stories about the Landlord. But I have been through Pagus in my rounds too often to think it was quite so simple. What really happened was this: The Landlord succeeded in getting a lot of messages through.'

'What sort of messages?'

'Mostly pictures. You see, the Pagans couldn't read, because the Enemy shut up the schools as soon as he took over Pagus. But they had pictures. The moment you mentioned your Island I knew what you were at. I have seen that Island dozens of times in those pictures.'

'And what happened then?'

'Almost certainly the same thing has happened to you. These pictures woke desire. You understand me?'

'Very well.'

'And then the Pagans made mistakes. They would keep on trying to get the same picture again: and if it didn't come, they would make copies of it for themselves. Or even if it did come they would try to get out of it not desire but satisfaction. But you must know all this.'

'Yes, yes, indeed. But what came of it?'

'They went on making up more and more stories for themselves about the pictures, and then pretending the stories were true. They turned to brown girls and tried to believe that that was what they wanted. They went far South, some of them and became magicians, and tried to believe it was that. There was no absurdity and no indecency they did not commit. But however far they went, the Landlord was too many for them. Just when their own stories seemed to have completely overgrown the original messages and hidden them beyond recovery, suddenly the Landlord would send them a new message and all their stories would look stale. Or just when they seemed to be growing really contented with lust or mystery mongering, a new message would arrive and the old desire, the real one, would sting them again, and they would say "Once more it has escaped us".'

'I know. And then the whole cycle would begin over again.'

'Yes. But all the while there was one people that could read. You have heard of the Shepherd People?'

'I had been hoping you would not come to that, Father. I have heard the Stewards talk of them and I think it is that more than anything else that sickened me of the whole story. It is so clear that the Shepherd People are just one of these Pagan peoples—and a peculiarly unattractive one. If the whole thing is hobbled by one leg to that special People . . .'

'This is merely a blunder,' said History. 'You, and those whom you trust, have not *travelled*. You have never been in Pagus, nor among the Shepherds. If you had lived on the roads as I have, you would never say that they were the same. The Shepherds could read: that is the thing to remember about them. And because they could read, they had from the Landlord, not pictures but Rules.'

'But who wants Rules instead of Islands?'

'That is like asking who wants cooking instead of dinner. Do you not see that the Pagans, because they were under the enemy, were beginning at the wrong end? They were like lazy schoolboys attempting eloquence before they learn grammar. They had pictures for their eyes instead of roads for their feet, and that is why most of them could do nothing but desire and then, through starved desire, become corrupt in their imaginations, and so awake and despair, and so desire again. Now the Shepherds, because they were under the Landlord, were made to begin at the right end. Their feet were set on a road: and as the

Landlord's Son once said, if the feet have been put right the hands and the head will come right sooner or later. It won't work the other way.'

'You know so much, Father,' said John, 'that I do not know how to answer you. But this is all unlike the accounts I have heard of those countries. Surely some of the Pagans did get somewhere.'

'They did. They got to Mother Kirk. That is the definition of a Pagan—a man so travelling that if all goes well he arrives at Mother Kirk's chair and is carried over this gorge. I saw it happen myself. But we define a thing by its perfection. The trouble about Pagus is that the perfect, and in that sense typical, Pagan, is so uncommon there. It must be so, must it not? These pictures—this ignorance of writing—this endless desire which so easily confuses itself with other desires and, at best, remains pure only by knowing what it does *not* want—you see that it is a starting point from which *one* road leads home and a thousand roads lead into the wilderness.'

'But were the Shepherds not just as bad in their own way? Is it not true that they were illiberal, narrow, bigoted?'

'They *were* narrow. The thing they had charge of was narrow: it was the Road. They found it. They sign-posted it. They kept it clear and repaired it. But you must not think I am setting them up against the Pagans. The truth is that a Shepherd is only half a man, and a Pagan is only half a man, so that neither people was well without the other, nor could either be healed until the Landlord's Son came into the country. And even so, my son, you will not be well until you have overtaken your fellow traveller who slept in my cell last night.'

'Do you mean Vertue?' said John.

'That was his name. I knew him though he did not tell me, for I know his family; and his father, whom he does not know, was called Nomos and lived among the Shepherds. You will never do anything until you have sworn blood brotherhood with him: nor can he do anything without you.'

'I would gladly overtake him,' said John, 'but he is so angry with me that I am afraid to come near him. And even if we made it up, I don't see how we could help falling out again. Somehow we have never been able to be quite comfortable together for very long.'

155

'Of yourselves you never will. It is only a third that can reconcile you.'

'Who is that?'

'The same who reconciled the Shepherds and the Pagans. But you must go to Mother Kirk to find him.'

'It is raining harder than ever,' said John from the mouth of the cave.

'It will not stop to-night,' said Father History. 'You must stay with me till the morning.'

CHAPTER NINE

Matter of Fact

'I SEE,' said John presently, 'that this question is harder than the Clevers and the pale men suppose. But they were right in distrusting the Island. From all that you have told me, it is a very dangerous thing.'

'There is no avoiding danger in our country,' said History. 'Do you know what happens to people who set about learning to skate with a determination to get no falls? They fall as often as the rest of us, and they cannot skate in the end.'

'But it is more than dangerous. You said it was beginning at the wrong end, while the Shepherd people began at the right end.'

'That is true. But if you are a Pagan by birth or by nature, you have no choice. It is better to begin at the wrong end than not to begin at all. And the most part of men are always Pagans. Their first step will always be the desire born of the pictures: and though that desire hides a thousand false trails it also hides the only true one for them, and those who preach down the desire under whatever pretext—Stoic, Ascetic, Rigorist, Realist, Classicist—are on the Enemy's side whether they know it or not.'

'Then there is always need for the Island?'

'It does not always take the form of an Island, as I have said. The Landlord sends pictures of many different kinds. What is universal is not the particular picture, but the arrival of some message, not perfectly intelligible, which wakes this desire and sets men longing for some-thing East or West of the world; something possessed, if at all, only in the act of desiring it, and lost so quickly that the craving itself becomes craved; something that tends inevitably to be confused with common or even with vile satisfactions lying close to hand, yet which is able, if any man faithfully live through the dialectic of its successive births and deaths, to lead him at last where true joys are to be found. As for the shapes in which it comes, I have seen many in my travels. In Pagus it was sometimes, as I said, an Island. But it was often, too, a picture of people, stronger and fairer than we are. Sometimes it was a picture telling a story. The strangest shape it ever took was in Medium Aevum —that was a master stroke of the Landlord's diplomacy; for of course, since the Enemy has been in the country, the Landlord has had to become a politician. Medium Aevum was first inhabited by colonists from Pagus. They came there at the very worst period in the history of Pagus, when the Enemy seemed to have succeeded completely in di-verting all the desires that the Landlord could arouse into nothing but lust. These poor colonists were in such a state that they could not let their fancies wander for a minute without seeing images of black, craving eyes, and breasts, and gnawing kisses. It seemed hopeless to do anything with them. Then came the Landlord's crowning audacity. The very next picture he sent them was a picture of a Lady! Nobody had ever had the idea of a Lady before: and yet a Lady is a woman: so this was a new thing, which took the Enemy off his guard, and yet at the same time it was an old thing—in fact, the very thing which he was reckoning on as his strongest point. He got the shock of his life. The people went mad over the new picture, and made songs that are sung still, and looked away from the picture at the real women around them and saw them quite differently—so that ordinary love for women became, for a time, itself a form of the real desire, and not merely one of the spurious satisfactions offered to it. Of course the Landlord was playing a dangerous game (nearly all his games *are* dangerous) and the Enemy managed to mix up and corrupt the new message—as usual— but not so much as he wished, or as people afterwards said: and before he had recovered himself, one at least[1] of the tenants had carried this

[1] Dante

157

new form of the desire right up to its natural conclusion and found
what he had really been wanting. He wrote it all down in what he
called a *Comedy*.'

'And what about Mr. Halfways?' said John. 'Where did his kind
of song begin?'

'That was the last big arrival of new messages that we had,' said
History. 'And it happened just before I retired from the world. It was
in the land of Mr. Enlightenment, but he was very different then. I do
not know any man who has deteriorated so with advancing years. In
those days Claptrap had not been built. The Enemy had agents in the
country but did not come there often himself: it must have been just
about that time that Mammon was taking it over, and building new
towns and turning the people out of the fields into the factories. One of
the results was a great deal of anæmia—though there were other causes
for that too—and weak hearts. This time the Landlord did a curious
thing: he sent them pictures of the country they were actually living in
—as if he had sent them a number of mirrors. You see, he always does
the last thing the Enemy is expecting. And just as the pictures of the
Lady in Medium Aevum had made the real women look different, so
when men looked at these pictures of the country and then turned to the
real landscape, it was all changed. And a new idea was born in their
minds, and they saw something—the old something, the Island West
of the world, the Lady, the heart's desire—as it were hiding, yet not
quite hidden, like something ever more about to be, in every wood and
stream and under every field. And because they saw this, the land
seemed to be coming to life, and all the old stories of the Pagans came
back to their minds and meant more than the Pagans themselves ever
knew: and because women also were in the landscape, the old idea of
the Lady came back too. For this is part of the Landlord's skill, that
when one message has died he brings it to life again in the heart of the
next. But out of this third revelation, which they called Romantic, so
many songs were made that I cannot remember all of them: and many
deeds were done, too, and many, through the usual false starts and dis-
illusions and rebeginnings of desire, found their way home. Your Mr.
Halfways is one of the later and weaker followers of that school.'

'I don't think that the history of the Romantic pictures is quite as clear as the other histories. What exactly was the Landlord doing? And what did the Enemy do?'

'I thought you would have seen. This third stroke of policy was in a way one of the greatest. All the previous pictures had been of something that was *not there* in the world around you. This gave the Enemy the chance of making people believe that you *had* it in the picture, and *lacked* it elsewhere—in other words that the picture itself was the thing you wanted. And that, as you know, means idolatry, and then, when the idol disappoints you (as it must) there is an easy passage to all the spurious satisfactions. But this weapon was knocked out of the Enemy's hand when once the thing in the picture was the very same thing that you saw all round you. Even the stupidest tenant could see that you *had* the landscape, in the only sense in which it could be had, already: and still you *wanted*: therefore the landscape was not what you wanted. Idolatry became impossible. Of course the Enemy when he had recovered himself, found a new method of defence. Just because the new message could not be idolized, it could be easily belittled. The desire awakened this between the picture and the countryside could be confused with the ordinary *pleasure* that any healthy man feels in moving about out-of-doors: and when it had been so confused, the Enemy could pretend that the Romantics had made a great pother about nothing. And you can imagine that all the people who had not had pictures sent to them, and therefore not felt the desire, and therefore were itching with envy, would welcome this explanation.'

'I see,' said John. 'But still—on your own showing, all these messages get blurred and corrupted in the end, and then, surely, the thing to do is to look out for the new one. These pale men might be quite right to occupy themselves in cleaning away the rubbish of the old revelation. That might be the way to get ready for the next.'

'That is another notion they have which a little travel would soon blow to pieces. They think that the Landlord works like the factories in Claptrap, inventing every day a new machine which supersedes the old. As machines are among the very few things that they do know something about, they cannot help thinking that everything is like them. But this leads them into two mistakes. First of all, they have no conception how slowly the Landlord acts—the enormous intervals between these big changes in his type of picture. And secondly, they think that the new thing refutes and cancels the old, whereas, in reality it brings it to a fuller life. I have never known a case where the man who was engaged in ridiculing or rejecting the old message became the receiver of the new. For one thing it all takes so long. Why, bless my soul, I remember Homer in Pagus ridiculing some of the story pictures: but they had thousands of years to run still and thousands of souls were to get nourishment out of them. I remember Clopinel[1] in Medium Aevum, jeering at the pictures of the Lady before they had reached half his countrymen. But his jeer was no spell to evoke a new message, nor was he helping any cause but the Enemy's.'

CHAPTER TEN

Archtype and Ectype

THERE was a long silence in the cave except for the sound of the rain. Then John began once more:

'And yet . . .' he said, 'and yet, Father, I am terribly afraid. I am afraid that the things the Landlord really intends for me may be utterly unlike the things he has taught me to desire.'

'They will be very unlike the things you imagine. But you already know that the objects which your desire imagines are always inad-equate to that desire. Until you have it you will not know what you wanted.'

'I remember that Wisdom said that too. And I understand that. Perhaps what troubles me is a fear that my desires, after all you have said, do not really come from the Landlord—that there is some older and rival Beauty in the world which the Landlord will not allow me to get. How can we *prove* that the Island comes from him? Angular would say it did not.'

'You have proved it for yourself: you have *lived* the proof. Has not every object which fancy and sense suggested for the desire, proved a failure, confessed itself, after trial, not to be what you wanted? Have

[1] Jean de Meung

160

you not found by elimination that this desire is the perilous siege in which only One can sit?'

'But, then,' said John, 'the very quality of it is so—so unlike what we think of the Landlord. I will confess to you what I had hoped to keep secret. It has been with me almost a bodily desire. There have been times . . . I have felt the sweetness flow over from the soul into the body . . . pass through me from head to foot. It is quite true, what the Clevers say. It *is* a thrill—a physical sensation.'

'That is an old story. You must fear thrills, but you must not fear them too much. It is only a foretaste of that which the real Desirable will be when you have found it. I remember well what an old friend of mine in Medium Aevum once said to me—"out of the soul's bliss," he said, "there shall be a flowing over into the flesh." '

'Did he say that? I did not suppose that anyone except the Clevers knew it. Do not laugh at me, Father—or laugh if you will—I am indeed very ignorant and I have listened to people more ignorant still.'

Twilight, hastened by the rain, had fallen on the canyon, and in the cave it was quite dark. John heard the old man moving to and fro and presently there came the flame of a little lamp lighting up his pale bird-like face. He set food for supper before his guest and bade him eat and then sleep.

'Gladly, Father,' said John, 'for I am very tired. I do not know why I have plagued you with questions about the Island. It is all a story of what happened to me long ago. It was long ago that I saw it clearly. The visions, ever since the first one, have grown rarer, the desires fainter. I have been talking as if I still craved it, but I do not think I can find any craving in my heart now at all.'

The old man sat still, nodding a little as before.

Suddenly John spoke again.

'Why should it *wear out* if it is from the Landlord? It doesn't last, you know. Isn't it that which gives away the whole case?'

'Have you not heard men say, or have you forgotten, that it is like human love?' asked the hermit.

'What has that to do with it?'

'You would not ask if you had been married, or even if you had studied generation among the beasts. Do you not know how it is with love? First comes delight: then pain: then fruit. And then there is joy of the fruit, but that is different again from the first delight. And mortal lovers must not try to remain at the first step: for lasting passion is the dream of a harlot and from it we wake in despair. You must not try to keep the raptures: they have done their work. Manna kept, is worms. But you are full of sleep and we had better talk no more.'

Then I dreamed that John lay down on a hard bed in the cave; and as he lay between waking and sleeping, the hermit, as he thought, lit two candles at the back of the cave on an altar and went to and fro doing and saying his holy things. And on the very borders of sleep John heard him begin to sing, and this was the song:

'My heart is empty. All the fountains that should run
    With longing, are in me
Dried up. In all my countryside there is not one
    That drips to find the sea.
I have no care for anything thy love can grant
    Except the moment's vain
And hardly noticed filling of the moment's want
    And to be free from pain.
Oh, thou that art unwearying, that dost neither sleep
    Nor slumber, who didst take
All care for Lazarus in the careless tomb, oh keep
    Watch for me till I wake.
If thou think for me what I cannot think, if thou
    Desire for me what I
Cannot desire, my soul's interior Form, though now
    Deep-buried, will not die,
—No more than the insensible dropp'd seed which grows
    Through winter ripe for birth
Because, while it forgets, the heaven remembering throws
    Sweet influence still on earth,
—Because the heaven, moved moth-like by thy beauty, goes
    Still turning round the earth.

BOOK NINE

ACROSS THE CANYON

Sholde nevere whete wexe bote whete fyrste deyde;
And other sedes also, in the same wyse,
That ben leide on louh erthe, ylore as hit were,
And thorwh the grete grace of God, of greyn ded in erthe
Atte last launceth up wher-by we liven alle.—LANGLAND

You will not sleep, if you lie there a thousand years, until you have opened your hand and yielded that which is not yours to give or to withhold. You may think you are dead, but it will be only a dream; you may think you have come awake, but it will still be only a dream. Open your hand, and you will sleep indeed—then wake indeed.
                                        —GEORGE MACDONALD

You may as well come quiet.—POLICE MAXIM

CHAPTER ONE

Across the Canyon by the Inner Light

WHEN John opened his eyes the day was still far off but there was light in the cave as though from a hundred candles. The hermit lay fast asleep by one wall of the cell as John lay by the other, and between them stood a woman, something like Reason and something like Mother Kirk, very bright.

'I am Contemplation,' she said. 'Rise and come with me.'

'You are not like the Contemplation that I know,' said John.

'It is one of my shadows whom you have met,' said the Lady. 'And there is little good in them and less harm. But rise and come.'

Then John rose and the Lady took him by the hand and led him out on to the ledge before the cave. And the night was still black with thunderous rain, but the lady and he were in a sphere of light, so that the raindrops as they passed out of the darkness into it became bright like diamonds in the centre of the sphere and iridescent at the circumference. Held by the Lady's hand he crossed the chasm and passed up the glens of the mountains on the other side. When they had travelled a long way (and still the darkness lay everywhere save where they trod) they came to the sea. And they crossed the sea also, gliding a little above the water, and the water also was dark until it reached their light, but within that it was blue as though it lay in Mediterranean sunshine. But presently the surrounding darkness vanished away and the drop of light in which they had journeyed entered an ocean of light and was swallowed up. The sky was visible above them and it seemed to be early morning, for it was cool and dew soaked their feet. And John looked and saw fields going up before him and the light ran down as a river in the midst of the fields, singing with a voice like a river but more articulate and very loud, too bright to look at. There were many people with them. And as John looked round upon the people he saw that they were approaching some high walls and great gates. And, at the shape of the towers clustered above him, a memory, very deeply buried, stirred in his mind, first sweet, then uneasy, then spreading through the pool of his mind in widening circles of dismay, till at last with certainty, inevitable, unbearable, there flashed before him the picture of those turreted crags seen long ago from Puritania at the summit of the Eastern mountains, and he saw where he was—beyond the brook—where Uncle George had vanished—at the Landlord's castle—the good kind Landlord with the black hole. He began to draw his hand out of the Lady's hand. He could not get it free. She was leading him on to the castle gates and all the crowd of people were moving on in the same direction, with a sinister happiness on their faces. He struggled with Contemplation and screamed: and with that and the struggling he awoke.

CHAPTER TWO

This Side by Lightning

IT was now pitchy black in the cave. Only the quiet breathing of the hermit recalled to John where he was: and with the first return of the knowledge he was already creeping out of the cave to dare the black night and the narrow ledge, to crawl the skin off his hands and his knees, to do and suffer anything so long as he was going back and not on—on in this direction where the next turning might lead him into the heart of his adversary's power. The rain fell in torrents and thunder echoed among the rocks: but the cool moisture on his back was better than the hot moisture on his forehead. He did not dare to stand up and walk, for the new terrors had not driven out the old, but rather joined with them in a phantasmagoric harmony, so that all in one moment his inner eye saw the black hole full of the spiders and scorpions—the narrow, narrow ledge sloping horribly the wrong way—the drop into the darkness and his own body bounced from crag to crag—the terrible face of Uncle George when the mask would not stay on it. And as the flashes came faster and the thunder followed faster on each flash, a new fear joined the dance: and in each flash the timeless unforgettable sight of the cliffs, lit up from end to end, gave a new edge to the old fear of climbing: and that again brought back the fear of Uncle George's face (so will mine look when I lie broken at the bottom of the gorge), until at last, when the complexity of fears seemed to admit no increase, a sharp, commanding voice out of the darkness suddenly startled him with such a shock that he seemed not to have been frightened till then.

'Back!' said the voice.

John crouched motionless from the balance of fears. He was not even sure that he *could* turn on this bit of the ledge.

'Back,' said the voice, 'or else show that you're the better man.'

. The lightning tore open the darkness and flung it to again. But John had seen his enemy. It was Reason, this time on foot, but still mailed, and her sword drawn in her hand.

'Do you want to fight?' she said in the darkness.

John had a wild thought of catching one of the mailed ankles from where he crouched: but when he had a picture of Reason falling into the gulf he could not get it clear of another picture in which he fell with her.

'I can't turn here,' he said: but the steel was at his throat and turn he did. He shuffled along at a surprising speed, still on his hands and knees, till he had passed the cave again. It was no longer a question of plans or of ultimate escape. The hunted animal's impulse to prolong the chase kept him ragingly on the move. The flashes were growing rarer and a star or two showed ahead. Then all of a sudden a wind shook the last raindrops fiercely in his face and there was moonlight all about him. But he drew back with a groan.

CHAPTER THREE

This Side by the Darkness

WITHIN an inch of him he had seen a face. Now a cloud crossed the moon and the face was no longer visible, but he knew that it was still looking at him—an aged, appalling face, crumbling and chaotic, larger than human. Presently its voice began:

'Do you still think it is the black hole you fear? Do you not know

even now the deeper fear whereof the black hole is but the veil? Do
you not know why they would all persuade you that there is nothing
beyond the brook and that when a man's lease is out his story is done?
Because, if this were true, they could in their reckoning make me equal
to nought, therefore not dreadful: could say that where I am they are
not, that while they are, I am not. They have prophesied soft things to
you. I am no negation, and the deepest of your heart acknowledges it.
Else why have you buried the memory of your uncle's face so carefully
that it has needed all these things to bring it up? Do not think that you
can escape me; do not think you can call me Nothing. To you I am
not Nothing; I am the being blindfolded, the losing all power of self-
defence, the surrender, not because any terms are offered, but because
resistance is gone: the step into the dark: the defeat of all precautions:
utter helplessness turned out to utter risk: the final loss of liberty. The
Landlord's Son who feared nothing, feared me.'

'What am I to do?' said John.

'Which you choose,' said the voice. 'Jump, or be thrown. Shut your
eyes or have them bandaged by force. Give in or struggle.'

'I would sooner do the first, if I could.'

'Then I am your servant and no more your master. The cure of death
is dying. He who lays down his liberty in that act receives it back. Go
down to Mother Kirk.'

John looked about him when next the moon shone. The bottom of
the chasm was level far below him, and there he saw what seemed a
concourse of dark figures. Amidst them they had left an open space,
where there was a glimmer as of water: and near the water there was
someone standing. It seemed to him that he was waited for, and he
began to explore the face of cliff below him. To his surprise it was no
longer sheer and smooth. He tried a few footholds and got five feet
below the ledge. Then he sat down again, sick. But the kind of fear
which he now suffered was cold and leaden: there was no panic in it:
and soon he continued his descent.

CHAPTER FOUR

Securus Te Projice

ON the floor of *Peccatum Adae* stood Mother Kirk crowned and sceptred in the midst of the bright moonlit circle left by the silent people. All their faces were turned towards her, and she was looking eastward to where John slowly descended the cliff. Not far from her sat Vertue, mother-naked. They were both on the margin of a large pool which lay in a semicircle against the western cliff. On the far side of the water that cliff rose sheer to the edge of the canyon. There was deep silence for about half an hour.

At last the small, drooping figure of a man detached itself from the shadow of the crags and advanced towards them through the open moonlight. It was John.

'I have come to give myself up,' he said.

'It is well,' said Mother Kirk. 'You have come a long way round to reach this place, whither I would have carried you in a few moments. But it is very well.'

'What must I do?' said John.

'You must take off your rags,' said she, 'as your friend has done already, and then you must dive into this water.'

'Alas,' said he, 'I have never learned to dive.'

'There is nothing to learn,' said she. 'The art of diving is not to do anything new but simply to cease doing something. You have only to let yourself go.'

'It is only necessary,' said Vertue, with a smile, 'to abandon all efforts at self-preservation.'

'I think,' said John, 'that if it is all one, I would rather jump.'

'It is not all one,' said Mother Kirk. 'If you jump, you will be trying to save yourself and you may be hurt. As well, you would not go deep enough. You must dive so that you can go right down to the bottom of the pool: for you are not to come up again on this side. There is a tunnel in the cliff, far beneath the surface of the water, and it is through that that you must pass so that you may come up on the far side.'

'I see,' thought John to himself, 'that they have brought me here to kill me,' but he began, nevertheless, to take off his clothes. They were little loss to him, for they hung in shreds, plastered with blood and with the grime of every shire from Puritania to the canyon: but they were so stuck to him that they came away with pain and a little skin came with them. When he was naked Mother Kirk bade him come to the edge of the pool, where Vertue was already standing. It was a long way down to the water, and the reflected moon seemed to look up at him from the depth of a mine. He had had some thought of throwing himself in, with a run, the very instant he reached the edge, before he had time to be afraid. And the making of that resolution had seemed to be itself the bitterness of death, so that he half believed the worst must be over and that he would find himself in the water before he knew. But lo! he was still standing on the edge, still on this side. Then a stranger thing came to pass. From the great concourse of spectators, shadowy people came stealing out to his side, touching his arm and whispering to him: and every one of them appeared to be the wraith of some old acquaintance.

First came the wraith of old Enlightenment and said, 'There's still time. Get away and come back to me and all this will vanish like a nightmare.'

Then came the wraith of Media Halfways and said, 'Can you really risk losing me for ever? I know you do not desire me at this moment. But for ever? Think. Don't burn your boats.'

And the wraith of old Halfways said, 'After all—has this anything to do with the Island as you used to imagine it? Come back and hear my songs instead. You *know* them.'

The wraith of young Halfways said, 'Aren't you ashamed? Be a man. Move with the times and don't throw your life away for an old wives' tale.'

The wraith of Sigmund said, 'You know what this is, I suppose. Religious melancholia. Stop while there is time, If you dive, you dive into insanity.'

The wraith of Sensible said, 'Safety first. A touch of rational piety adds something to life: but this salvationist business . . . well! Who knows where it will end? Never accept unlimited liabilities.'

The wraith of Humanist said, 'Mere atavism. You are diving to escape your real duties. All this emotionalism, after the first plunge, is so much *easier* than virtue in the classical sense.'

The wraith of Broad said, 'My dear boy, you are losing your head. These sudden conversions and violent struggles don't achieve anything. We have had to discard so much that our ancestors thought necessary. It is all far easier, far more gracious and beautiful than they supposed.'

But at that moment the voice of Vertue broke in:

'Come on, John,' he said, 'the longer we look at it the less we shall like it,' And with that he took a header into the pool and they saw him no more. And how John managed it or what he felt I did not know, but he also rubbed his hands, shut his eyes, despaired, and let himself go. It was not a good dive, but, at least, he reached the water head first.

CHAPTER FIVE

Across the Canyon

My dream grew darker so that I have a sense, but little clear memory of the things that John experienced both in the pool and in great catacombs, paved sometimes with water, sometimes with stone, and upon winding stairways in the live rocks whereby he and Vertue ascended through the inwards of the mountain to the land beyond *Peccatum Adae*. He learned many mysteries in the earth and passed through many elements, dying many deaths. One thing has come through into my waking memory. Of all the people he had met in his journey only Wisdom appeared to him in the caverns, and troubled him by saying that no man could really come where he had come and that all his adventures were but figurative, for no professed experience of these places could be anything other than mythology. But then another voice spoke to him from behind him, saying:

'Child, if you will, it *is* mythology. It is but truth, not fact: an image, not the very real. But then it is My mythology. The words of Wisdom are also myth and metaphor: but since they do not know themselves for what they are, in them the hidden myth is master, where it should be servant: and it is but of man's inventing. But this is My inventing, this is the veil under which I have chosen to appear even from the first until now. For this end I made your senses and for this end your imagi-nation, that you might see My face and live. What would you have? Have you not heard among the Pagans the story of Semele? Or was there any age in any land when men did not know that corn and wine were the blood and body of a dying and yet living God?'

And not long after that the light and colour, as with the sound of a trumpet, rushed back upon my dreaming eyes, and my ears were full of the sounds of bird and the rustle of leaves, for John and Vertue had come up out of the earth into the green forests of the land beyond the canyon. Then I saw that they were received into a great company of other pilgrims who had all descended like them into the water and the earth and again come up, and now took their march westward along the banks of a clear river. All kinds of men were among them. And during the whole of this part of their journey Reason rode with the company, talking to them at will and not visiting them any longer by sudden starts, nor vanishing suddenly. It was a wonder to John to find so many companions: nor could he conceive how he had failed to run across them in the earlier parts of his journey.

I watched this journey in my dream a long time. At the outset their goal was heard of only by rumours as of something very far off: then, by continuous marching, winding their way among the peaked and valleyed lands, I saw where they came down to the white beaches of a bay of the sea, the western end of the world; a place very ancient, folded many miles deep in the silence of forests; a place, in some sort, lying rather at the world's beginning, as though men were born travelling away from it. It was early in the morning when they came there and heard the sound of the waves; and looking across the sea—at that hour still almost colourless—all these thousands became still. And what the others saw I do not know: but John saw the Island. And the morning wind, blowing off-shore from it, brought the sweet smell of its orchards to them, but rarefied and made faint with the thinness and purity of early air, and mixed with a little sharpness of the sea. But for John, because so many thousands looked at it with him, the pain and the longing were changed and all unlike what they had been of old: for humility was mixed with their wildness, and the sweetness came not with pride and with the lonely dreams of poets nor with the glamour of a secret, but with the homespun truth of folk-tales, and with the sadness of graves and freshness as of earth in the morning. There was fear in it also, and hope: and it began to seem well to him that the Island should be different from his desires, and so different that, if he had known it, he would not have sought it.

CHAPTER SIX

Nella sua Voluntade

How it fared with the other pilgrims I did not see, but presently a comely person took John and Vertue apart and said that he had been appointed to be their Guide. I dreamed that he was one born in the Mountain and they called him Slikisteinsauga because his sight was so sharp that the sight of any other who travelled with him would be sharpened by his company.

'Thank you,' said John. 'Pray, do we take ship from here?'

But Slikisteinsauga shook his head: and he asked them to look at the Island again and specially to consider the shape of the crags, or the castle (for they could not well see which at that distance) to which it rose at its highest point.

'I see,' said John presently.

'What do you see?' said the Guide.

'They are the very same shape as that summit of the Eastern Mountain which we called the Landlord's castle as we saw it from Puritania.'

'They are not only the same shape. They are the same.'

'How can that be?' said John with a sinking heart, 'for those mountains were in the extreme East, and we have been travelling West ever since we left home.'

172

'But the world is round,' said the Guide, 'and you have come nearly round it. The Island is the Mountains: or, if you will, the Island is the other side of the Mountains, and not, in truth, an Island at all.'

'And how do we go on from here?'

The Guide looked at him as a merciful man looks on an animal which he must hurt.

'The way to go on,' he said at last, 'is to go back. There are no ships. The only way is to go East again and cross the brook.'

'What must be must be,' said John. 'I deserve no better. You mean that I have been wasting my labour all my life, and I have gone half-round the world to reach what Uncle George reached in a mile or so.'

'Who knows what your uncle has reached, except the Landlord? Who knows what you would have reached if you had crossed the brook without ever leaving home? You may be sure the Landlord has brought you the shortest way: though I confess it would look an odd journey on a map.'

'How does it strike you, friend?' said John to Vertue.

'It cannot be helped,' said Vertue. 'But indeed, after the water and the earth, I thought we had already crossed the brook in a sense.'

'You will be always thinking that,' said the Guide. 'We call it Death in the Mountain language. It is too tough a morsel to eat at one bite. You will meet that brook more often than you think: and each time you will suppose that you have done with it for good. But some day you really will.'

They were all silent for a while.

'Come,' said the Guide at last, 'if you are ready let us start East again. But I should warn you of one thing—the country will look very different on the return journey.

BOOK TEN

THE REGRESS

And if, when he returned into the cave, he were constrained once more to contend with those that had always there been prisoners, in judgment of the said shadows, would they not mock him, and say of him that by going up out of the cave he had come down again with his eyes marred for his pains, and that it was lost labour for any so much as to try that ascent?—PLATO

First I must lead the human soul through all the range
Of heaven, that she may learn
How fortune hath the turning of the wheel of change,
How fate will never turn.—BERNARDUS SILVESTRIS

Let us suppose a person destitute of that knowledge which we have from our senses ... Let it be supposed that in his drought he puts golden dust into his eyes: when his eyes smart, he puts wine into his ears; that in his hunger, he puts gravel into his mouth; that in pain, he loads himself with the iron chains: that feeling cold, he puts his feet in the water; that being frighted at the fire, he runs away from it; that being weary, he makes a seat of his bread.... Let us suppose that some good being came to him, and showed him the nature and use of all the things that were about him.—LAW

CHAPTER ONE

The Same yet Different

THEN I dreamed that the Guide armed John and Vertue at all points and led them back through the country they had just been travelling, and across the canyon again into this country. And they came up out of the canyon at the very place where the main road meets it by Mother Kirk's chair. I looked forward in the same direction where they were looking, expecting to see on my left the bare tableland rising to the North with Sensible's house a little way off, and on my right the house of Mr. Broad and the pleasant valleys southward. But there was nothing of the kind: only the long straight road, very narrow, and on the left crags rising within a few paces of the road into ice and mist and, beyond that, black cloud: on the right, swamps and jungle sinking almost at once into black cloud. But, as it happens in dreams, I never doubted that this was the same country which I had seen before, although there was no similarity. John and Vertue came to a stand with their surprise.

'Courage,' said Slikisteinsauga, 'you are seeing the land as it really is. It is long but very narrow. Beyond these crags and cloud on the North it sinks immediately into the Arctic Sea, beyond which again lies the Enemy's country. But the Enemy's country is joined up with ours on the North by a land bridge called the Isthmus Sadisticus and right amid that Isthmus sits the cold dragon, the cold, costive, crustacean dragon who wishes to enfold all that he can get within the curl of his body and then to draw his body tighter round it so as to have it all inside himself. And you, John, when we pass the Isthmus must go up and contend with him that you may be hardened. But on the South, as soon as it passes into these swamps and this other cloud, the land sinks into the Southern Sea: and across that sea also there comes a land bridge, the Isthmus Mazochisticus, where the hot dragon crawls, the expansive, invertebrate dragon whose fiery breath makes all that she touches melt and corrupt. And to her you, Vertue, must go down that you may steal her heat and be made malleable.'

176

'Upon my soul,' said John, 'I think Mother Kirk treats us very ill. Since we have followed her and eaten her food the way seems twice as narrow and twice as dangerous as it did before.'

'You all know,' said the Guide, 'that security is mortals' greatest enemy.'

'It will do very well,' said Vertue, 'let us begin.'

Then they set out on their journey and Vertue sang this song:

> 'Thou only art alternative to God, oh, dark
> And burning island among spirits, tenth hierarch,
> Wormwood, immortal Satan, Ahriman, alone
> Second to Him to whom no second else were known,
> Being essential fire, sprung of His fire, but bound
> Within the lightless furnace of thy Self, bricked round
> To rage in the reverberated heat from seven
> Containing walls: hence power thou hast to rival heaven.
> Therefore, except the temperance of the eternal love
> Only thy absolute lust is worth the thinking of.
> All else is weak disguisings of the wishful heart,
> All that seemed earth is Hell, or Heaven. God is: thou art:
> The rest, illusion. How should man live save as glass
> To let the white light without flame, the Father, pass
> Unstained: or else—opaque, molten to thy desire,
> Venus infernal starving in the strength of fire!'

'Lord, open not too often my weak eyes to this.'

CHAPTER TWO

The Synthetic Man

As they went on, Vertue glanced to the side of the road to see if there were any trace of Mr. Sensible's house, but there was none.

'It is just as it was when you passed it before,' said the Guide, 'but your eyes are altered. You see nothing now but realities: and Mr.

177

Sensible was so near to nonentity—so shadowy even as an appearance—that he is now invisible to you. That mote will trouble your eyes no longer.

'I am very surprised,' said Vertue, 'I should have thought that even if he was bad he was a singularly solid and four-square kind of evil.

'All that solidity,' said the Guide, 'belonged not to him but to his predecessors in that house. There was an appearance of temperance about him, but it came from Epicurus. There was an appearance of poetry, but it came from Horace. A trace of old Pagan dignities lingered in his house—it was Montaigne's. His heart seemed warm for a moment, but the warmth was borrowed from Rabelais. He was a man of shreds and patches, and when you have taken from him what was not his own, the remainder equals nought.'

'But surely,' said Vertue, 'these things were not the less his own because he learned them from others.'

'He did not learn them. He learned only catchwords from them. He could talk like Epicurus of spare diet, but he was a glutton. He had from Montaigne the language of friendship, but no friend. He did not even know what these predecessors had really said. He never read one ode of Horace seriously in his life. And for his Rabelais, he can quote *Do what you will*. But he has no notion that Rabelais gave that liberty to his Thelemites on the condition that they should be bound by Honour, and for this reason alone free from laws positive. Still less does he know that Rabelais himself was following a great Steward of the olden days who said *Habe caritatem et fac quod vis*: and least of all that this Steward in his turn was only reducing to an epigram the words of his Master, when He said, "On these two commandments hang all the law and the prophets."'

CHAPTER THREE

Limbo

THEN I dreamed that John looked aside on the right hand of the road and saw a little island of willow trees amid the swamps, where ancient men sat robed in black, and the sound of their sighing reached his ears.

'That place,' said the Guide, 'is the same which you called the Valley of Wisdom when you passed it before: But now that you are going East you may call it Limbo, or the twilit porches of the black hole.'

'Who live there?' asked John, 'and what do they suffer?'

'Very few live there, and they are all men like old Mr. Wisdom—men who have kept alive and pure the deep desire of the soul but through some fatal flaw, of pride or sloth or, it may be, timidity, have refused till the end the only means to its fulfilment; taking huge pains, often, to prove to themselves that the fulfilment is impossible. They are very few because old Wisdom has few sons who are true to him, and the most part of those who come to him either go on and cross the canyon, or else, remaining his sons in name, secretly slip back to feed on worse fare than his. To stay long where he lives requires both a strange strength and a strange weakness. As for their sufferings, it is their doom to live for ever in desire without hope.'

'Is it not rather harsh of the Landlord to make them suffer at all?'

'I can answer that only by hearsay,' returned the Guide, 'for pain is a secret which he has shared with your race and not with mine; and you would find it as hard to explain suffering to me as I should find it to reveal to you the secrets of the Mountain people. But those who know best say this, that any liberal man would choose the pain of this desire, even for ever, rather than the peace of feeling it no longer: and that though the best thing is to have, the next best is to want, and the worst of all is not to want.'

'I see that,' said John, 'Even the wanting, though it is pain too, is more precious than anything else we experience.'

'It is as I foresaw, and you understand it already better than I can. But there is this also. The Landlord does not condemn them to lack of hope: they have done that themselves. The Landlord's interference is all on the other side. Left to itself, the desire without the hope would soon fall back to spurious satisfactions, and these souls would follow it of their own free will into far darker regions at the very bottom of the black hole. What the Landlord has done is to fix it forever: and by

179

his art, though unfulfilled, it is uncorrupted. Men say that his love and his wrath are one thing. Of some places in the black hole you cannot see this, though you can believe it: but of that Island yonder under the willows, you can see it with your own eyes.'

'I see it very well,' said John.

Then the Guide sang:

> 'God in His mercy made
> The fixèd pains of Hell.
> That misery might be stayed,
> God in His mercy made
> Eternal bounds and bade
> Its waves no further swell.
> God in his mercy made
> The fixèd pains of Hell.'

CHAPTER FOUR

The Black Hole

'THEN there is, after all,' said John, 'a black hole such as my old Steward described to me.'

'I do not know what your Steward described. But there is a black hole.'

'And still the Landlord is "so kind and good"!'

'I see you have been among the Enemy's people. In these latter days there is no charge against the Landlord which the Enemy brings so often as cruelty. That is just like the Enemy: for he is, at bottom, very dull. He has never hit on the one slander against the Landlord which would be really plausible. Anyone can refute the charge of cruelty. If he really wants to damage the Landlord's character, he has a much stronger line than that to take. He ought to say that the Landlord is an inveterate gambler. That would not be true, but it would be plausible, for there is no denying that the Landlord does take risks.'

'But what about the charge of cruelty?'

'I was just coming to that. The Landlord has taken the risk of working the country with free tenants instead of slaves in chain gangs: and as they are free there is no way of making it impossible for them to go into forbidden places and eat forbidden fruits. Up to a certain point he can doctor them even when they have done so, and break them off the habit. But beyond that point—you can see for yourself. A man can go on eating mountain-apple so long that *nothing* will cure his craving for it: and the very worms it breeds inside him will make him more certain to eat more. You must not try to fix the point after which a return is impossible, but you can see that there will be such a point somewhere.'

'But surely the Landlord can do anything?'

'He cannot do what is contradictory: or, in other words, a meaningless sentence will not gain meaning simply because someone chooses to prefix to it the words "the Landlord can". And it is meaningless to talk of forcing a man to do freely what a man has freely made impossible for himself.'

'I see. But at least these poor creatures are unhappy enough: there is no need to add a black hole.'

'The Landlord does not make the blackness. The blackness is there already wherever the taste of mountain-apple has created the vermiculate will. What do you mean by a hole? Something that ends. A black hole is blackness enclosed, limited. And in that sense the Landlord *has* made the black hole. He has put into the world a Worst Thing. But evil of itself would never reach a worst: for evil is fissiparous and could never in a thousand eternities find any way to arrest its own reproduction. If it could, it would be no longer evil: for Form and Limit belong to the good. The walls of the black hole are the tourniquet on the wound through which the lost soul else would bleed to a death she never reached. It is the Landlord's last service to those who will let him do nothing better for them.'

Then the Guide sang:

'Nearly they stood who fall;
Themselves as they look back
See always in the track
The one false step, where all

181

Even yet, by lightest swerve
Of foot not yet enslaved,
By smallest tremor of the smallest nerve,
Might have been saved.

'Nearly they fell who stand,
And with cold after fear
Look back to mark how near
They grazed the Sirens' land,
Wondering that subtle fate,
By threads so spidery fine,
The choice of ways so small, the event so great,
Should thus entwine.

'Therefore oh, man, have fear
Lest oldest fears be true,
Lest thou too far pursue
The road that seems so clear,
And step, secure, a hair's
Breadth past the hair-breadth bourne,
Which, being once crossed forever unawares,
Denies return.'

CHAPTER FIVE

Superbia

THEN they went further and saw in the rocks beside them on the left what seemed at first sight a skeleton, but as they drew nearer they saw that there was indeed skin stretched over its bones and eyes flaming in the sockets of its skull. And it was scrabbling and puddering to and fro on what appeared to be a mirror; but it was only the rock itself scraped clean of every speck of dust and fibre of lichen and polished by the continued activity of this famished creature.

'This is one of the Enemy's daughters,' said the Guide, 'and her

182

name is Superbia. But when you last saw her, perhaps she wore the
likeness of three pale men.'

As they passed her she began to croak out her song.

> 'I have scraped clean the plateau from the filthy earth,
> Earth the unchaste, the fruitful, the great grand maternal,
> Sprawling creature, lolling at random and supine
> The broad-faced, sluttish helot, the slave wife
> Grubby and warm, who opens unashamed
> Her thousand wombs unguarded to the lickerous sun.
> Now I have scoured my rock clean from the filthy earth,
> On it no root can strike and no blade come to birth,
> And though I starve of hunger it is plainly seen
> That I have eaten nothing common or unclean.
>
> 'I have by fasting purged away the filthy flesh,
> Flesh the hot, moist, salt scum, the obscenity
> And parasitic tetter, from my noble bones.
> I have torn from my breasts—I was an udder'd beast—
> My child, for he was fleshly. Flesh is caught
> By a contagion carried from impure
> Generation to generation through the body's sewer.
> And now though I am barren, yet no man can doubt
> I am clean and my iniquities are blotted out.
>
> 'I have made my soul (once filthy) a hard, pure, bright
> Mirror of steel: no damp breath breathes upon it
> Warming and dimming: it would freeze the finger
> If any touched it. I have a mineral soul.
> Minerals eat no food and void no excrement.
> So I, borrowing nothing and repaying
> Nothing, neither growing nor decaying,
> Myself am to myself, a mortal God, a self-contained
> Unwindowed monad, unindebted and unstained.'

John and the Guide were hurrying past, but Vertue hesitated.

'Her means may be wrong,' he said, 'but there is something to be
said for her idea of the End.'

'What idea?' said the Guide.

'Why—self-sufficiency, integrity. Not to commit herself, you know. All said and done, there *is* something foul about all these natural processes.'

'You had better be careful of your thoughts here,' said the Guide. 'Do not confuse Repentance with Disgust: for the one comes from the Landlord and the other from the Enemy.'

'And yet disgust has saved many a man from worse evils.'

'By the power of the Landlord it may be so—now and then. But don't try to play that game for yourself. Fighting one vice with another is about the most dangerous strategy there is. You know what happens to kingdoms that use alien mercenaries.'

'I suppose you are right,' said Vertue, 'and yet this feeling goes very deep. Is it wholly wrong to be ashamed of being in the body?'

'The Landlord's Son was not. You know the verses—"When thou tookest upon thee to deliver man".'

'That was a special case.'

'It was a special case because it was the archtypal case. Has no one told you that that Lady spoke and acted for all that bears, in the presence of all that begets: for this country as against the things East and West: for matter as against form and patiency against agency? Is not the very word Mother akin to Matter? Be sure that the whole of this land, with all its warmth and wetness and fecundity with all the dark and the heavy and the multitudinous for which you are too dainty, spoke through her lips when she said that He had regarded the lowliness of His hand-maiden. And if that Lady was a maid though a mother, you need not doubt that the nature which is, to human sense, impure, is also pure.'

'Well,' said Vertue, turning away from Superbia, 'I will think this over.'

'One thing you may as well know,' remarked the Guide, 'whatever virtues you may attribute to the Landlord, decency is not one of them. That is why so few of your national jokes have any point in my country.'

And as they continued their journey, Vertue sang:

> 'Because of endless pride
> Reborn with endless error,

184

The vision of God is the fountain of Humility

Each hour I look aside
Upon my secret mirror
Trying all postures there
To make my image fair.

'Thou givest grapes, and I,
Though starving, turn to see
How dark the cool globes lie
In the white hand of me,
And linger gazing thither
Till the live clusters wither.

'So should I quickly die
Narcissus-like of want,
But, in the glass, my eye
Catches such forms as haunt
Beyond nightmare, and make
Pride humble for pride's sake.

'Then and then only turning
The stiff neck round, I grow
A molten man all burning
And look behind and know
Who made the glass, whose light makes dark,
    whose fair
Makes foul, my shadowy form reflected there
That Self-Love, brought to bed of Love may
    die and bear
Her sweet son in despair.'

CHAPTER SIX

Ignorantia

STILL I lay dreaming and saw these three continue their journey
through that long and narrow land with the rocks upon their left and

the swamps on their right. They had much talk on the way of which I have remembered only snatches since I woke. I remember that they passed Ignorantia some miles beyond her sister Superbia and that led the pilgrims to question their Guide as to whether the Ignorance of the Tough-minded and the Clevers would some day be cured. He said there was less chance of that now than there had ever been: for till recently the Northern people had been made to learn the languages of Pagus 'and that meant', said the Guide, 'that at least they started no further from the light than the old Pagans themselves and had therefore the chance to come at last to Mother Kirk. But now they are cutting themselves off even from that roundabout route.'

'Why have they changed?' asked one of the others.

'Why did the shadow whom you call Sensible leave his old house and go to practise αὐτάρκεια in a hotel? Because his Drudge revolted. The same thing is happening all over the plateau and in Mammon's country: their slaves are escaping further north and becoming dwarfs, and therefore the masters are turning all their attention to machinery, by which they hope to be able to lead their old life without slaves. And this seems to them so important that they are suppressing every kind of knowledge except mechanical knowledge. I am speaking of the sub-tenants. No doubt the great landowners in the back-ground have their own reasons for encouraging this movement.'

'There must be a good side somewhere to this revolution,' said Vertue. 'It is too solid—it looks too lasting—to be a mere evil. I cannot believe that the Landlord would otherwise allow the whole face of nature and the whole structure of life to be so permanently and radically changed.'

The Guide laughed. 'You are falling into their own error,' he said, 'the change is not radical, nor will it be permanent. That idea depends on a curious disease which they have all caught—an inability to dis-believe advertisements. To be sure, if the machines did what they promised, the change would be very deep indeed. Their next war, for example, would change the state of their country from disease to death. They are afraid of this themselves—though most of them are old enough to know by experience that a gun is no more likely than a toothpaste or a cosmetic to do the things its makers say it will do. It is the same with all their machines. Their labour-saving devices multiply drudgery; their aphrodisiacs make them impotent: their amusements bore them: their rapid production of food leaves half of them starving, and their devices for saving time have banished leisure from their country. There will be no radical change. And as for permanence—consider how quickly all machines are broken and obliterated. The black solitudes will some day be green again, and of all cities that I have seen these iron cities will break most suddenly.'

And the Guide sang:

> 'Iron will eat the world's old beauty up.
> Girder and grid and gantry will arise,
> Iron forest of engines will arise,
> Criss-cross of iron crotchet. For your eyes
> No green or growth. Over all, the skies
> Scribbled from end to end with boasts and lies.
> (When Adam ate the irrevocable apple, Thou
> Saw'st beyond death the resurrection of the dead.)

> 'Clamour shall clean put out the voice of wisdom,
> The printing-presses with their clapping wings,
> Fouling your nourishment. Harpy wings,
> Filling your minds all day with foolish things,
> Will tame the eagle Thought: till she sings
> Parrot-like in her cage to please dark kings.
> (When Israel descended into Egypt, Thou
> Didst purpose both the bondage and the coming out.)

> 'The new age, the new art, the new ethic and thought,
> And fools crying, Because it has begun
> It will continue as it has begun!
> The wheel runs fast, therefore the wheel will run
> Faster for ever. The old age is done,
> We have new lights and see without the sun.
> (Though they lay flat the mountains and dry up the sea,
> Wilt thou yet change, as though God were a god?)'

CHAPTER SEVEN

Luxuria

AFTER this, John looked up and saw that they were approaching a concourse of living creatures beside the road. Their way was so long and desolate (and he was footsore too) that he welcomed any diversion, and he cast his eyes curiously upon this new thing. When he was nearer he saw that the concourse was of men, but they lay about in such attitudes and were so disfigured that he had not recognized them for men: moreover, the place was to the south of the road, and therefore the ground was very soft and some of them were half under water and some hidden in the reeds. All seemed to be suffering from some disease of a crumbling and disintegrating kind. It was doubtful whether all the life that pulsated in their bodies was their own: and soon John was certain, for he saw what seemed to be a growth on a man's arm slowly detach itself under his eyes and become a fat reddish creature, separable from the parent body, though it was in no hurry to separate itself. And once he had seen that, his eyes were opened and he saw the same thing happening all round him, and the whole assembly was but a fountain of writhing and reptilian life quickening as he watched and sprouting out of the human forms. But in each form the anguished eyes were alive, sending to him unutterable messages from the central life which survived, self-conscious, though the self were but a fountain of vermin. One old cripple, whose face was all gone but the mouth and eyes, was sitting up to receive drink from a cup which a woman held to his lips. When he had as much as she thought good, she snatched the cup from his hands and went on to her next patient. She was dark but beautiful.

'Don't lag,' said the Guide, 'this is a very dangerous place. You had better come away, This is Luxuria.'

But John's eyes were caught by a young man to whom the witch had just come in her rounds. The disease, by seeming, had hardly begun with him: there was an unpleasant suspicion about his fingers—something a little too supple for joints—a little independent of his other movements—but, on the whole, he was still a well-looking person. And as the witch came to him the hands shot out to the cup, and the man drew them back again: and the hands went crawling out for the cup a second time, and again the man wrenched them back, and turned his face away, and cried out:

'Quick! The black, sulphurous, never quenched,
Old festering fire begins to play
Once more within. Look! By brute force I have wrenched
Unmercifully my hands the other way.

'Quick, Lord! On the rack thus, stretched tight,
Nerves clamouring as at nature's wrong.
Scorched to the quick, whipp'd raw—Lord, in this plight
You see, you see no man can suffer long.

'Quick, Lord! Before new scorpions bring
New venom—ere fiends blow the fire
A second time—quick, show me that sweet thing
Which, 'spite of all, more deeply I desire.'

And all the while the witch stood saying nothing, but only holding out the cup and smiling kindly on him with her dark eyes and her dark, red mouth. Then, when she saw that he would not drink, she passed on to the next: but at the first step she took, the young man gave a sob and his hands flew out and grabbed the cup and he buried his head in it: and when she took it from his lips clung to it as a drowning man to a piece of wood. But at last he sank down in the swamp with a groan. And the worms where there should have been fingers were unmistakable.

'Come on,' said Vertue.

They resumed their journey, John lagging a bit. I dreamed that the witch came to him walking softly in the marshy ground by the roadside and holding out the cup to him also: when he went faster she kept pace with him.

'I will not deceive you,' she said. 'You see there is no pretence. I am not trying to make you believe that this cup will take you to your

Island. I am not saying it will quench your thirst for long. But taste it, none the less, for you are very thirsty.'

But John walked forward in silence.

'It is true,' said the witch, 'that you never can tell when you have reached the point beyond which there is no return. But that cuts both ways. If you can never be certain that one more taste is safe, neither can you be certain that one more taste is fatal. But you can be certain that you are terribly thirsty.'

But John continued as before.

'At least,' said the witch, 'have one more taste of it, before you abandon it for ever. This is a bad moment to choose for resistance, when you are tired and miserable and have already listened to me too long. Taste this once, and I will leave you. I do not promise never to come back: but perhaps when I come again you will be strong and happy and well able to resist me—not as you are now.'

And John continued as before.

'Come,' said the witch. 'You are only wasting time. You know you will give in, in the end. Look ahead at the hard road and the grey sky. What other pleasure is there in sight?'

So she accompanied him for a long way, till the weariness of her importunity tempted him far more than any positive desire. But he forced his mind to other things and kept himself occupied for a mile or so by making the following verses:

> When Lilith means to draw me
> Within her secret bower,
> She does not overawe me
> With beauty's pomp and power,
> Nor, with angelic grace
> Of courtesy, and the pace
> Of gliding ships, comes veiled at evening hour.
>
> Eager, unmasked, she lingers
> Heart-sick and hunger sore;
> With hot, dry, jewelled fingers
> Stretched out, beside her door,
> Offering with gnawing haste

Her cup, whereof who taste,
(She promises no better) thirst far more.

What moves me, then, to drink it?
—Her spells, which all around
So change the land, we think it
A great waste where a sound
Of wind like tales twice told
Blusters, and cloud is rolled
Always above yet no rain falls to ground.

Across drab iteration
Of bare hills, line on line,
The long road's sinuation
Leads on. The witch's wine,
Though promising nothing, seems
In that land of no streams,
To promise best—the unrelished anodyne.

And by the time he had reached the word *anodyne* the witch was gone. But he had never in his life felt more weary, and for a while the purpose of his pilgrimage woke no desire in him.

CHAPTER EIGHT

The Northern Dragon

'Now,' said the Guide, 'our time is come.'

They looked at him inquiringly.

'We are come,' said he, 'to that point of the road which lies midway between the two land bridges that I spoke of. The cold dragon is here on our left, and the hot dragon on our right. Now is the time to show what you are made of. Wolf is waiting in the wood southward: in the rocks northward, raven wheeling, in hope of carrion. Behoves you both be on guard quickly. God defend you.'

'Well,' said Vertue. And he drew his sword and slung his shield round from his back. Then he held out his hand first to the Guide, and then to John. 'So long,' he said.

'Go where it is least green,' said Guide, 'for there the ground is firmest. And good luck.'

Vertue left the road and began to pick his way cautiously southward, feeling out the fen-paths. The Guide turned to John.

'Have you any practice with a sword?' he said.

'None, sir,' answered John.

'None is better than a smattering. You must trust to mother-wit. Aim at his belly—an upward jab. I shouldn't try cutting, if I were you: you don't know enough.'

'I will do the best I can,' said John. And then, after a pause: 'There is only one dragon, I suppose. I don't need to guard my back.'

'Of course there is only one, for he has eaten all the others. Otherwise he would not be a dragon. You know the maxim—*serpens nisi serpentem comederit*——'

Then I saw John also settle his gear and step off the road to the left. The ascent began at once, and before he was ten yards from the road he was six feet above it: but the formation of the rocks was such that it was like mounting a huge stair, and was tiring rather than difficult. When he first stopped to wipe the sweat out of his eyes the mist was already so dense that he could hardly see the road beneath him. Ahead the grey darkness shaded quickly into black. Then suddenly John heard a dry, rattling sound in front of him, and a little above. He got a better grip on his sword, and took one pace towards it, listening intently. Then came the sound again: and after that he heard a croaking voice, as of a gigantic frog. The dragon was singing to himself:

'Once the worm-laid egg broke in the wood.
I came forth shining into the trembling wood,
The sun was on my scales, dew upon the grasses,
The cool, sweet grasses and the budding leaves.
I wooed my speckled mate. We played at druery
And sucked warm milk dropping from the goats' teats.

'Now I keep watch on the gold in my rock cave
In a country of stones: old, deplorable dragon,

Watching my hoard. In winter night the gold
Freezes through toughest scales my cold belly.
The jagged crowns and twisted cruel rings
Knobbly and icy are old dragon's bed.

'Often I wish I hadn't eaten my wife,
Though worm grows not to dragon till he eat worm.
She could have helped me, watch and watch about,
Guarding the hoard. Gold would have been the safer.
I could uncoil my weariness at times and take
A little sleep, sometimes when she was watching.

'Last night under the moonset a fox barked,
Woke me. Then I knew I had been sleeping.
Often an owl flying over the country of stones
Startles me, and I think I must have slept.
Only a moment. That very moment a man
Might have come out of the cities, stealing, to get my gold.

'They make plots in the towns to steal my gold.
They whisper of me in a low voice, laying plans,
Merciless men. Have they not ale upon the benches,
Warm wife in bed, singing, and sleep the whole night?
But I leave not the cave but once in winter
To drink of the rock pool: in summer twice.

'They feel no pity for the old, lugubrious dragon.
Oh, Lord, that made the dragon, grant me Thy peace!
But ask not that I should give up the gold,
Nor move, nor die; others would get the gold.
Kill, rather, Lord, the men and the other dragons
That I may sleep, go when I will to drink.'

As John listened to this song he forgot to be afraid. Disgust first,
and then pity, chased fear from his mind: and after them came a strange
desire to speak with the dragon and to suggest some sort of terms and
division of the spoil: not that he desired the gold, but it seemed to him a
not all ignoble desire to surround and contain so much within oneself.

But while these things passed through his imagination, his body took care of him, keeping his grip steady on the sword hilt, his eyes strained into the darkness, and his feet ready to spring: so that he was not taken by surprise when he saw that in the rolling of the mist above him something else was rolling, and rolling round him to enclose him. But still he did not move. The dragon was paying its body out like a rope from a cave just above him. At first it swayed, the great head bobbing vertically, as a caterpillar sways searching for a new grip with half its length while the other half rests still on the leaf. Then the head dived and went behind him. He kept turning round to watch it, and it led the volume of the dragon's body round in a circle and finally went back into the cave, leaving a loop of dragon all round the man. Still John waited till the loop began to tighten, about on a level with his chest. Then he ducked and came up again with a jab of his sword into the under-side of the brute. It went in to the hilt, but there was no blood. At once the head came twisting back out of the cave. Eyes full of cruelty—cold cruelty without a spark of rage in it—stared into his face. The mouth was wide open—it was not red within, but grey like lead—and the breath of the creature was freezing cold. As soon as it touched John's face, everything was changed. A corselet of ice seemed to be closed about him, seemed to shut in his heart, so that it could never again flutter with panic or with greed. His strength was multiplied. His arms seemed to him iron. He found he was laughing and making thrust after thrust into the brute's throat. He found that the struggle was already over—perhaps hours ago. He was standing unwearied in a lonely place among rocks with a dead reptile at his feet. He remembered that he had killed it. And the time before he had killed it seemed very long ago.

CHAPTER NINE

The Southern Dragon

JOHN came leaping down the rocks into the road, whistling a tune. The Guide came to greet him, but before they had spoken a word they, both turned round in wonder at a great cry from the South. The sun had come out so that the whole marsh glittered like dirty copper: and at first they thought that it was the sun upon his arms that made Vertue flash like flame as he came leaping, running, and dancing towards them. But as he drew nearer they saw that he was veritably on fire. Smoke came from him, and where his feet slipped into the bog holes there were little puffs of steam. Hurtless flames ran up and down his sword and licked over his hand. His breast heaved and he reeled like a drunk man. They made towards him, but he cried out:

'I have come back with victory got—
But stand away—touch me not
Even with your clothes. I burn red-hot.

'The worm was bitter. When she saw
My shield glitter beside the shaw
She spat flame from her golden jaw.

'When on my sword her vomit spilt
The blade took fire. On the hilt
Beryl cracked, and bubbled gilt.

'When sword and sword arm were all flame
With the very heat that came
Out of the brute, I flogged her tame.

'In her own spew the worm died.
I rolled her round and tore her wide
And plucked the heart from her boiling side,

'When my teeth were in the heart
I felt a pulse within me start
As though my breast would break apart.

'It shook the hills and made them reel
And spun the woods round like a wheel.
The grass singed where I set my heel.

'Behemoth is my serving man!
Before the conquered hosts of Pan

> Riding tamed Leviathan,
> Loud I sing for well I can
> RESVRGAM and IO PAEAN,
> Io, Io, Io, PAEAN!!

> 'Now I know the stake I played for,
> Now I know what a worm's made for!'

CHAPTER TEN

The Brook

MY dream was full of light and noise. I thought they went on their way singing and laughing like schoolboys. Vertue lost all his dignity, and John was never tired: and for ten miles or so they picked up an old fiddler who was going that way, who played them such jigs and they danced more than they walked. And Vertue invented doggerels to his tunes to mock the old Pagan virtues in which he had been bred.

But in the midst of all this gaiety, suddenly John stood still and his eyes filled with tears. They had come to a little cottage, beside a river, which was empty and ruinous. Then they all asked John what ailed him.

'We have come back to Puritania,' he said, 'and that was my father's house. I see that my father and mother are gone already beyond the brook. I had much I would have said to them. But it is no matter.'

'No matter indeed,' said the Guide, 'since you will cross the brook yourself before nightfall.'

'For the last time?' said Vertue.

'For the last time,' said the Guide, 'all being well.'

And now the day was declining and the Eastern Mountains loomed big and black ahead of them. Their shadows lengthened as they went down towards the brook.

'I am cured of playing the Stoic,' said Vertue, 'and I confess that I go down in fear and sadness. I also—there were many people I would have spoken to. There were many years I would call back. Whatever there is beyond the brook, it cannot be the same. Something is being ended. It is a real brook.

> 'I am not one that easily flits past in thought
> The ominous stream, imagining death made for nought.
> This person, mixed of body and breath, to which concurred
> Once only one articulation of thy word,
> Will be resolved eternally: nor can time bring
> (Else time were vain) once back again the self-same thing.
> Therefore among the riddles that no man has read
> I put thy paradox, Who liveth and was dead.
> As Thou hast made substantially, thou wilt unmake
> In earnest and for everlasting. Let none take
> Comfort in frail supposal that some hour and place
> To those who mourn recovers the wished voice and face.
> Whom Thy great *Exit* banishes, no after age
> Of epilogue leads back upon the lighted stage.
> Where is Prince Hamlet when the curtain's down?
>   Where fled
> Dreams at the dawn, or colours when the light is sped?
> We are thy colours, fugitive, never restored,
> Never repeated again. Thou only art the Lord,
> Thou only art holy. In the shadowy vast
> Of thine Osirian wings Thou dost enfold the past.
> There sit in throne antediluvian, cruel kings,
> There the first nightingale that sang to Eve yet sings,
> There are the irrecoverable guiltless years,
> There, yet unfallen, Lucifer among his peers.
>
> 'For thou art also a deity of the dead, a god
> Of graves, with necromancies in thy potent rod;
> Thou art Lord of the unbreathable transmortal air
> Where mortal thinking fails: night's nuptial darkness, where
> All lost embraces intermingle and are bless'd,
> And all die, but all are, while Thou continuest.'

The twilight was now far advanced and they were in sight of the brook. And John said, 'I thought all those things when I was in the house of Wisdom. But now I think better things. Be sure it is not for nothing that the Landlord has knit our hearts so closely to time and place—to one friend rather than another and one shire more than all the land.

> 'Passing to-day by a cottage, I shed tears
> When I remembered how once I had dwelled there
> With my mortal friends who are dead. Years
> Little had healed the wound that was laid bare.
>
> 'Out, little spear that stabs. I, fool, believed
> I had outgrown the local, unique sting,
> I had transmuted away (I was deceived)
> Into love universal the lov'd thing.
>
> 'But Thou, Lord, surely knewest Thine own plan
> When the angelic indifferences with no bar
> Universally loved but Thou gav'st man
> The tether and pang of the particular;
>
> 'Which, like a chemic drop, infinitesimal,
> Plashed into pure water, changing the whole,
> Embodies and embitters and turns all
> Spirit's sweet water to astringent soul.
>
> 'That we, though small, may quiver with fire's same
> Substantial form as Thou—nor reflect merely,
> As lunar angel, back to thee, cold flame.
> Gods we are, Thou has said: and we pay dearly.'

And now they were already at the brook, and it was so dark that I did not see them go over. Only, as my dream ended, and the voice of the birds at my window began to reach my ear (for it was a summer morning), I heard the voice of the Guide, mixed with theirs and not unlike them, singing this song:

> 'I know not, I,
>   What the men together say,
> How lovers, lovers die
>   And youth passes away.

The Angel sings

'Cannot understand
  Love that mortal bears
For native, native land
  —All lands are theirs.

'Why at grave they grieve
  For one voice and face,
And not, and not receive
  Another in its place.

'I, above the cone
  Of the circling night
Flying, never have known
  More or lesser light.

'Sorrow it is they call
  This cup: whence my lip,
Woe's me, never in all
  My endless days must sip.'

CPSIA information can be obtained
at www.ICGtesting.com
Printed in the USA
BVHW052317110623
665785BV00003B/27

9 781014 151704